D1553877

STORIES
AT
WORK

Hi Doug,

Hope to meet you someday

soon.

Story on!

Icy.

22 SEP 2018

'The secret sauce to inspirational leadership is storytelling. Learning to tell stories based on real business experiences can ignite the imagination and transform other businesses. That's where *Stories at Work* . . . works!'—Anand Kripalu, managing director and CEO, United Spirits Limited

'We are never too old for stories. And in business, storytelling drives shared values and organizational culture. This book is a delightful introduction to this most important leadership skill'—Anand Mahindra, chairman, Mahindra Group

'I saw first-hand the power of stories three years ago when Indranil helped us craft and narrate stories for one of our transformation initiatives. This is a delightful book full of insights, tools and techniques that can help leaders learn and practise this powerful leadership skill'—Bhargav Dasgupta, managing director and CEO, ICICI Lombard

'Storytelling has been a buzzword of late but has remained steeped in mystery. This is the first book that makes it simple and learnable. I recommend this as a must-read for all those aspiring to be in positions of influence'—Krish Shankar, executive vice president and group head, human resource development, Infosys

'Facts and data don't shift behaviours. Stories do. I believe stories are a powerful tool to change cultures, to live values. Indranil is a master storyteller and I would recommend his book to anyone interested in driving change and transformation'—Leena Nair, chief human resource officer, Unilever

'Bullet points and opinions never inspire and are quickly forgotten. But stories are remembered, always inspire and have a tendency to spread. This book tells you how to communicate with clarity using storytelling—a powerful leadership skill'—Mukul Deoras, chief marketing officer, Colgate–Palmolive

'If you've ever wondered how you could communicate with more impact, look no further. This book is a simple, practical guide to potentially transformational outcomes'—Nitin Paranjpe, president, food and refreshments, Unilever

'In a simple and memorable way, Indranil brings to life the power of storytelling. Not just the why, but also the how. I highly recommend this book to anyone who is looking to communicate with impact' —Prabir Jha, president and global chief people officer, Cipla

'In human communication, facts talk to the mind. Emotions and context warm the heart. Storytelling combines fact, emotion and context. Storytelling is a human evolutionary inheritance—no different from language, rationality and standing on two legs rather than four! Yet humans need to relearn the skill. Indranil explains how . . . a worthy read'—R. Gopalakrishnan, corporate adviser and author of *A Biography of Innovations* and *What the CEO Really Wants from You*

'I was in the audience at a seminar when I heard Indranil speak about the power of stories in business. At the end of the allotted hour, I realized that I had not checked my phone even once. This book holds the promise of engaging your attention completely and mindfully' —Rama Bijapurkar, management consultant and author of *We Are like That Only* and *A Never-Before World*

'I have known Indranil for two decades. He has taught the principles of storytelling in every company where I was a chief executive officer and that helped us. He was also a regular speaker at AIMA retreats' —Shiv Shivakumar, group executive president, Aditya Birla Group

'*Stories at Work* is a great read for everyone as it brings to life the magical moments of engagement you can create through storytelling. Your authentic story is the most potent force that you can use to connect, engage and inspire'—Srikanth Balachandran, global chief human resource officer, Airtel

'Indranil's book comes at a time when organizations are coping with information overload and attention deficiency. In this, the casualty is individual alignment with the organization's goals. That "alignment" is a mental process. Neurologically speaking, it involves paying attention to something, liking it, remembering it and then following it.

Thus, we have to build memorability for the message and it is only possible through the narrative. The CEO of the future is a master narrator'—Subroto Bagchi, co-founder, Mindtree, and author of *Sell: The Art, the Science, the Witchcraft* and *On Leadership and Innovation*

'Through my career as a business journalist I have discovered that the best companies, CEOs and managers are invariably those that have the best stories. I am delighted to see Indranil's popular column in *Mint* progressing to a book'—Sukumar Ranganathan, editor-in-chief, *Hindustan Times*

STORIES

AT
WORK

UNLOCK THE SECRET TO
BUSINESS STORYTELLING

FOREWORD BY PIYUSH PANDEY

INDRANIL
CHAKRABORTY

PORTFOLIO
PENGUIN

An imprint of Penguin Random House

PORTFOLIO

USA | Canada | UK | Ireland | Australia
New Zealand | India | South Africa | China

Portfolio is part of the Penguin Random House group of companies
whose addresses can be found at global.penguinrandomhouse.com

Published by Penguin Random House India Pvt. Ltd
7th Floor, Infinity Tower C, DLF Cyber City,
Gurgaon 122 002, Haryana, India

Penguin
Random House
India

First published in Portfolio by Penguin Random House India 2018

Copyright © Indranil Chakraborty 2018
Foreword copyright © Piyush Pandey 2018
Prologue copyright © Shawn Callahan 2018

10 9 8 7 6 5 4 3 2 1

The views and opinions expressed in this book are the author's own and the
facts are as reported by him which have been verified to the extent possible,
and the publishers are not in any way liable for the same.

ISBN 9780670089840

Typeset in Adobe Jenson Pro by Manipal Digital Systems, Manipal
Printed at Replika Press Pvt. Ltd, India

www.penguin.co.in

MIX
Paper from
responsible sources
FSC® C016779

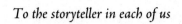

To the storyteller in each of us

CONTENTS

FOREWORD

'Tell me a fact and I'll learn. Tell me a truth and I'll believe.
But tell me a story and it will live in my heart forever.'

—an ancient North American Indian proverb

THIS IS THE power of a story—the power to touch the heart and be remembered. I have been in the business of advertising for over thirty-five years and have seen storytelling transform the fortunes of brands and businesses. Stories have the power to charm and influence and even change behaviour. It is stories that turn products into brands, which is the secret behind the iconicity of brands like Nike and Fevicol.

Our lives are actually a series of stories happening to each one of us. As a storyteller, one of my biggest sources of inspiration has been life—the life I have lived and the life around me. Adults turning into kids at Disneyland and toyshops inspired Cadbury's 'real taste of life' campaign. My father's constant refrain that he had to study under the street lights, which egged my brother and me on to become responsible and study using the many facilities and conveniences our generation had access to, stimulated a story for the launch of the Telugu newspaper *Sakshi*. 'What will I do with diamonds at this age?' my mother's statement when my brother and I gifted her diamond earrings, became a story for SBI Life Insurance Company. A prank my brother played in the parking lot of a five-star hotel found its way into a Sprite commercial. We store our memories in the form of visuals and as stories. As creative people, we retrieve some of them to tell stories.

However, my experience in the world of advertising shows that stories are not the domain of the creative mind alone. Interesting stories come to the fore when we talk to consumers about brands and their associations with them, and consumers play them back quite effortlessly. A chocolate lover once said that, during lunch, she shared her food with friends. But she waited for everyone to disperse before taking out her chocolate and eating it by herself as dessert. A fast-food brand loyalist spoke about how 'service-oriented' the brand was by narrating a story of how he saw the restaurant replace the meal of a patron when he slipped, no questions asked. One tea brand consumer from New Delhi recounted stories from her childhood about how her mother used to make tea for her while she studied during the early winter mornings. For another brand, the story was entirely different—how tea was served on a tray to guests—painting different images for the two brands in play. Clearly, when we investigate strengths and ideas to build brands, stories are a rich source of material that help to understand the emotions and feelings associated with it.

As children, stories are an essential part of life. We learn a lot of 'truths' through stories, especially in India. Values are

inculcated through the epics—Ramayana and Mahabharata—
and other stories like in *Panchatantra*. As children, between
siblings and friends, we indulge in play by weaving stories,
often building off each other's narratives and enjoying the
fantasy. However, once we start learning 'facts' in school, the
process of decline of stories begins. Stories, primarily in the
form of films and fiction, become entertainment. This finds
its way into adult life too. At work, in the name of *moti baat*,
or cutting to the chase, we move towards becoming more pithy
and concise in our communication, leaving out the richness
of what stories can reveal or provide. The PowerPoint
presentation is the final nail in the coffin of storytelling!
Interestingly, in everyday conversation, when we want to
share our emotions with family and friends—any of the nine
emotions outlined in the *Natyashastra*—we do it through
stories. We share happiness or sadness, fear or wonder, hate
or anger by describing 'events' that we have experienced or
seen around us, which are essentially stories.

In that context, this book of IC's is particularly interesting.
IC has had a background in marketing, which exists on the
foundation of storytelling. In the last few years, he has used
storytelling to conduct extensive training sessions across
organizations to unlock its power. So, he is best suited to share
his ideas on the subject.

The book itself eggs us on to get back to storytelling
and use it in everyday business. Whether it is to evangelize
a culture within an organization (for a CEO), understand
an employee's views about the brand (for human resources)
or interpret the consumers and customers (for sales and
marketing), storytelling can be a very effective tool. This book

helps you understand what a story is, why it is powerful and how it can be used to further a business's interests.

I am sure you will find this book both enjoyable and enriching.

Happy reading!

Piyush Pandey
executive chairman and creative director,
Ogilvy (South Asia)

PROLOGUE

URSULA LLABRES, A senior customer success manager at Yammer, had just ten minutes to communicate her message to 200 sales representatives of Microsoft.

Microsoft had acquired Yammer, an enterprise social networking service, in 2012. Her objective was to help Microsoft Office 365 'black belts' understand the value and impact of Yammer.

Llabres shared two customer stories. During a day packed with back-to-back sessions, her presentation stood out from the rest.

'It was the only talk all day where people closed their laptops and listened,' said Steve Hopkins, director of customer success (Australia), Yammer.

When Llabres finished, hands shot up with questions and Microsoft requested a follow-on impromptu Yammer 101 session for later that day. Representatives approached Llabres with more questions and requests to connect on Yammer. The approach Llabres and her colleagues took to prepare and deliver their messages varied significantly from the other speakers that day.

'We had just finished training with Anecdote and I used storytelling techniques to show the audience what we do and how we impact customers,' said Llabres.

Llabres is not alone. Over the last fifteen years, we have seen over 5000 participants go through our programme. Many of them have shared with us the almost instantaneous impact of the new skill they learnt. One example that comes to mind was during a programme we were running for Wrigley Company in Shanghai. One of the participants had a very high-stake meeting with government officials to demand a refund the day after the training programme. She had used that situation as an example during the practice session. She then applied the storytelling techniques she learnt during the meeting and was successful. I remember Catherine Pemberton, corporate affairs director (Pacific region) at Wrigley Company, telling me, 'The net result was that, by the end of the day, the training had already paid for itself—many times over.'

Effective leaders are good storytellers. I say 'good' because a leader merely has to share a story or two to set them apart from the rest, and most leaders communicate entirely with opinion and lofty abstractions. A leader's message really sticks when he or she illustrates points through a real-life experience, i.e., a story.

I saw a beautiful example of how it can be done a couple of years ago when I was helping the leaders of an insurance firm be better storytellers. The company had just appointed a new chief executive officer (CEO) who wanted to address the 100-odd people at the workshop I was facilitating.

When the CEO arrived, he shook hands with me and introduced himself to the audience. Within a couple of minutes, he had told them his first story about how he started his career in commercial insurance in the UK and the terrifying job he had of assessing assets atop power station cooling towers. This was his connection story. He was demonstrating how he was a little bit like his audience, that he had some understanding of their world.

He followed this up with an anecdote about a company where he was on the executive team, how they hit a cash crisis and the tough decisions that had to be made. He never wanted to be in that position again. He was making it clear what was important to him, sharing what he valued.

In fifteen minutes, this CEO shared a few more stories that helped everyone know what kind of a person he was, what he cared about and what really motivated him to take on this new role.

We had just seen a masterclass in leadership storytelling.

Now, some might say, 'Well, yes, he's clearly a natural storyteller. But for me storytelling just doesn't come that easily.' Let's think about this. Cast your mind back to your first business presentation. Can you remember it? I can certainly remember mine and I have to say that it didn't come easily. But I learnt how to present in front of a business audience with practice. You can learn to be a good storyteller. After all, the expert was a beginner once.

Having observed over two dozen business storytelling trainers across the world in action, I am convinced that the best trainers have at least two things in common. First, they are great storytellers themselves and, second, they are people with a background in business and who have led teams in large organizations.

Anyone teaching business storytelling must be proficient at telling business stories. Storytelling is a craft learnt through imitation and practice. Just like good writers are good readers, good storytellers are great story-listeners.

Leaders in large organizations should learn business storytelling from people who have worked in large organizations. Teachers with corporate experience understand the culture and constraints as well as the opportunities corporate life offers for business storytelling. This experience helps both the teacher and journeyman speak the same language.

In both these areas—being a great storyteller and being a leader in a large organization—IC (Indranil Chakraborty) scores head-and-shoulders above any other trainer that I have worked with. No wonder he is our most successful partner and a dear friend. He is someone we trust implicitly and who provides exemplary learning experiences to his clients.

I met Indranil in September 2012, when my business partner, Mark Schenk, and I travelled to New Delhi to run a 'Storytelling for Leaders' programme at The Oberoi Hotel in Gurgaon. Among the participants was Indranil Chakraborty, who everyone called 'IC'. He was then the chief marketing officer at Mahindra Holidays and was struggling to embed some newly articulated values into the organization. After the workshop, he invited Mark and me to have a drink with him at the hotel's bar. IC was planning the next step in his career and was excited about starting his own story business. Soon after that meeting, IC quit his corporate life and became our partner in India. What a great journey we've had over the last five years! When he reached out to me to seek permission to share with the world what he had learnt from us and what he had successfully used to convert over 1500 leaders into powerful storytellers, I couldn't have been happier.

He has captured all that we taught him and more. He has brought his unique blend of the left and right brain, and his wonderful sense of humour into a book which teaches as much as it entertains.

Stories at Work will light a fire in the imaginations of business leaders across India. Whether it's through helping leaders influence and inspire their people, shift to better organizational cultures, improve engagement, or one of the hundreds of other ways in which stories can make a difference to business, this book will become the dog-eared and underlined companion of the very best Indian leaders.

Melbourne

June 2018

Shawn Callahan

co-founder of Anecdote

ACKNOWLEDGEMENTS

I met Shawn Callahan and Mark Schenk from Anecdote Australia in the winter of 2012. They opened my eyes so wide to the power of stories in business that six months later I quit my twenty-one-year-old corporate career and knocked on their door to become a partner.

Their support, advice and encouragement has got me where I am today.

For the first forty-five years of my life, the only things I had written were emails and proposals. This is why when Indrajit Gupta, the co-founder of Founding Fuel, asked me to write an article on storytelling, I hesitated. This book wouldn't have happened without his conviction that storytelling in business is a skill that would benefit everybody and, of course, his belief that I too could write. One article followed the next and the readers' response encouraged me to continue. While the thought of writing a book on the subject had crossed my mind, I am sure it would never have happened unless Lohit Jagwani, my editor, hunted me down. This followed a year of guidance and gentle persuasion. The result was this book.

'Should I gift you a copy of Wren and Martin?' and 'I pity the person who has to copy-edit your book.' These were the constant refrains from my soulmate, life partner and travel companion who also doubles up as my legally wedded wife, Sabari, as she painstakingly read the book and gave me feedback which has made the book so much easier to read.

The day creative demigod and Padma Shri awardee Piyush Pandey agreed to write the foreword I was beside myself with joy. So, thank you Piyush! Also, a thank you to all the people who, without hesitance, agreed to read an advance copy of the book and share their thoughts: Anand Kripalu, Anand Mahindra, Bhargav Dasgupta, Krish Shankar, Leena Nair, Mukul Deoras, Nitin Paranjpe, Prabir Jha, R. Gopalakrishnan, Rama Bijapurkar, Shiv Shivakumar, Srikanth Balachandran, Subroto Bagchi and Sukumar Ranganathan.

Last but not the least I am thankful to my two four-legged children—Zara the pugnacious pug and Zen, the large-hearted golden retriever—without whose presence this book would have been completed several months ago, but our lives would have been poorer without their unconditional love.

INTRODUCTION

The Art of Gathering Gold Dust

IT WAS HOT and dusty, a typical summer's day in a small town in Uttar Pradesh. As a young sales manager at Hindustan Unilever, I was on my mandatory market visit. Today was the wholesale beat. Most of the wholesalers were working on a wafer-thin margin. Their way of working seemed to defy everything I had learnt at IIM (Indian Institute of Management) Ahmedabad. I sat on an empty oil tin, sipping a cup of tea made mostly of milk and sugar. I noticed a fifteen-year-old boy manning the store in his father's absence. I was in a good mood, so I decided to give him some commercial advice.

'You shouldn't be selling our products so cheap. By only keeping 0.5 per cent margin you will soon go out of business,' I said.

The young boy smiled.

'Sir, I don't think you understand. I make a lot of money from your products. Let me explain. I sell on cash.

I have about two weeks of stock, but I also get a week's credit from your distributor. This means that I essentially have a net investment of one week. My investment rotates fifty-two times in a year and with 0.5 per cent margin in each rotation, that is a return on investment (ROI) of 26 per cent. What's wrong with a 26 per cent ROI?' he spoke with the kind of panache usually expected from a VC-funded entrepreneur.

I was stumped. It was nothing short of an epiphany. What the uneducated young wholesaler had just taught me was how money is made by rotating money and not by the absolute amount of money earned in each transaction. It's like a wheel that turns very fast. And every time it turns, it picks up a little bit of gold dust, and that way the gold dust keeps accumulating.

I will never forget that lesson in my life. Very often you learn from the most unexpected sources.

These are not my words. This was sometime in 1992 when, as a management trainee, I remember listening with a lot of interest as Mukul Deoras, then a marketing manager at Hindustan Unilever, narrated this story. I remember sitting hunched over my notebook and furiously taking notes. He made a simple point. Don't let vanity come in the way. Important life lessons can come from anywhere. The fact that this lesson has stuck with me for over twenty-five years is not only a reflection of the impact of the message but also the way it was conveyed.

Using stories to convey a message is a powerful technique. Over the years, I have used it intuitively. It would have just been a skill, if not for a curious set of events starting 2011, the year that turned this conviction into a way of life and indeed my vocation too.

In 2011, I was appointed as the chief marketing officer of India's largest timeshare company, Mahindra Holidays. My team and I had just completed the exercise of creating a new vision for the company. Along with this, we had also articulated four desired employee behaviours or values. The vision was 'to make every moment magical' for our members. The expected behaviours were:

1. No room for ordinary (ordinary is not magical).
2. Experience is everything.
3. Make smiles.
4. Proud of our club.

This vision and the supporting values were very well received, especially by the seniors in the organization. But when the euphoria of having identified these fancy, flowery and hopefully inspiring values died down, I was left with the uncomfortable feeling that this may have been just another esoteric exercise that would only result in a plaque on a boardroom wall.

I started wondering. Just because the people at our head office got it, is it a given that employees who worked in far-flung corners of India would get it too?

Anxious to address this, I read whatever I could find on the subject of embedding values. I also discussed this with consultants and experts. I went ahead and did a few things which may seem foolish in hindsight. For example, I wrote to the 'contact us' email IDs of a few companies whose CEOs in some interview or the other had mentioned the importance of values. In these mails, I asked what they had done to embed the same. Most companies didn't respond. The few that did sent me annual reports and company brochures.

In the end, I was no wiser. So I did what I guess most people in my position do—I ran workshops designed to share Mahindra Holidays's new vision and values with the company's top 500 managers.

However, six months after the workshops, my travels across the country showed that we were in the same position as most other companies. Only a smattering of people could tell me what the values were, but even they were not very clear about what these really meant and what behaviour they would need to display on a day-to-day basis.

My quest to make these values come alive for employees took an interesting turn when serendipity connected me to Shawn Callahan and Mark Schenk, the founders of Anecdote, an Australian company that had been focused on something called 'business storytelling' for over ten years. 'Business' and 'storytelling' were two words whose individual meaning I knew but didn't realize the power of using them together effectively.*

At a mind-opening workshop conducted by them, I learnt about 'story listening', an art of drawing out stories

---

* Shawn Callahan, *Putting Stories to Work: Mastering Business Storytelling* (Australia: Pepperberg Press, 2016).

   Shawn describes in detail, through his decade of experience in the subject, the power of stories in business. With his permission, I have borrowed from his book and the workshops designed by him in my work and indeed in this book.

from people. I learnt that broadcasting stories collected from employees, which correctly reflect the desired behaviour, was a great way to embed values.

When I returned from the workshop, I launched into story-listening work. I taught people in the resorts to spot and report stories of our new values being lived. As the stories started pouring in, my excitement started rising.

Some contributions were forgettable:

'The guest asked me for an extra towel, so I gave him one and hence I lived the value "make smiles".'

Not a strong example, right? But then there were stories like the one mentioned below which changed my belief in them. It was not just an influential communication medium but the most powerful tool in a leader's arsenal for connecting, aligning and inspiring his/her team.

A receptionist at the Mahindra Holidays resort in Coorg, Karnataka, received a call from a member who was stuck in traffic on the way to the resort. The member was worried that he would not be able to check-in before the resort's restaurant ended its lunch service. He did not want his children to go hungry. So he requested that some food be kept aside for his family.

As the receptionist relayed this message to the restaurant, a colleague asked, 'Hey! Did you check with them about the route they were taking?'

When the receptionist told him which route it was, his colleague jokingly said, 'Pack some tea and cake with the lunch, they will take a long time to reach. That road has been blocked anticipating the arrival of the chief minister to inaugurate the local flower show.'

The worried receptionist muttered 'there are kids in the car'. Half an hour later, when his shift was over, without telling anyone, the receptionist loaded four lunch boxes on to his motorcycle.

Revving his bike through small lanes for about 12 km, he kept calling the member's mobile phone until he finally reached the car. He handed over the packets and said, 'Your children must be hungry.'

That is 'no room for ordinary' in action.

Within days of this story being shared, other similar inspiring stories started coming in. These stories showed that Mahindra Holidays's employees were living these values.

The story of the receptionist had breathed life into the formerly abstract line 'no room for ordinary'. I am sure that no amount of presentations, speeches, oaths, leaflets, banners, posters or screen savers could have got this message across as powerfully.

This experience of embedding values through stories converted me from being a seller of holidays to an evangelizer of the power of stories in business. Stories work!

While we will spend time in a later chapter on the science behind why stories work, here is a glimpse. Paul Zak is a neuro-economist—someone who applies neuroscience to understand the decision-making process of consumers. His work shows how stories can change brain chemistry, how moving stories generate chemicals like cortisol and oxytocin which can lead to unexpected behavioural changes, including profound acts of altruism.

In a lab experiment, Paul and his colleagues showed a set of people a very moving film about a father struggling to cope with his son's impending death due to cancer. A matched set of people were shown a film about the same father and son enjoying a day at the zoo. After viewing the video, three things were measured— the participants' oxytocin levels in the blood, their self-reported empathy and their desire to donate to a related charity.

The study came up with three main findings. First, viewing an emotional video raised oxytocin levels by an average of 47 per cent over baseline compared to those who watched an emotionally neutral video. Second, there was a positive relationship between the degree of empathy experienced and the change in oxytocin levels. Third, an increase in experienced empathy was associated with greater generosity.[1]

Of the participants who watched the emotionally charged video, 32 per cent made a monetary contribution.

Scary, manipulative power of stories? Of course. And that is why leaders using stories need to have their moral compass firmly pointing to true north. We will explore this in more depth in the chapter on ethics and business storytelling.

The power of stories that helps us connect, engage, gain insight and inspire is what I have been helping individuals and organizations to harness. Over the last five years, we have worked together to unleash this power in diverse areas like making messages stick, embedding values, understanding messy people issues, new ways of generating consumer insights and managing knowledge. And we are still uncovering the power of storytelling in business.

Since you are reading this, you are clearly curious about how this process works. We have all come across leaders who have captured our imagination through stories. A brilliant example of this is Steve Jobs's commencement address at Stanford in June 2015. He started the speech with 'I am honoured to be with you today at your commencement from one of the finest universities in the world. I never graduated from college. Truth be told, this is the closest I've ever gotten to a college graduation. Today I want to tell you three stories from my life. That's it. No big deal. Just three stories.' He then went on to tell three stories. The first was about connecting the dots, the second was about love and loss, and the third was about death.

He started the third with, 'When I was seventeen, I read a quote that went something like: "If you live each day as if it was your last, someday you'll most certainly be right." It made an impression on me, and since then, for the past thirty-three years, I have looked into the mirror every morning and asked myself: "If today were the last day of my life, would I want to do what I am about to do today?" And whenever the answer has been "no" for too many days in a row, I know I need to change something.'

This may be the most powerful commencement speech ever given not only at Stanford but anywhere else. And surely it was the most memorable ever. Anyone who has ever heard it remembers more of this speech than any other commencement speech they have heard. Many quote the famous last words: Stay Hungry. Stay Foolish.

This book is designed to take you from being a believer of the power of stories to a seasoned user of stories in business, first by introducing you to the various elements of story work and then sharing with you the process you can use to unlock this enormous potential.

However, to do that I must first shift a belief most people have about stories. Imagine that you are one among ten people sitting in a conference room waiting for a very important meeting to start and someone in the room says 'let me tell you a story'. Pause and think about what would be the first thing that would go through your mind. Take a minute.

If you are like 95 per cent of the 1500-plus senior leaders that I have run into during my workshops, your first thought would be along the line—'why is he wasting our time', 'it's time to be serious', 'what an idiot', 'has he not prepared for this', 'how long will this take' or 'why do I have to listen to it'. Very few of you, the 5 per cent, would say 'I want to know what he has to say' or 'I hope it is interesting.' That is the barrier stories face in business.

Most of you who have been in sales, and many of you who have not, would have at some point in time in the past been told by your boss '*Kahaani mat batao!*' (Don't tell me a story), when you were genuinely trying to explain the real reasons behind why something didn't happen. Most people label stories as being made up, something to be used for entertainment or something usually for children.

While this myth will surely be shattered as we journey through the book, it would be useful to introduce you to my definition of business storytelling. *Story is a fact. What we will do is wrap it in context and deliver it with emotion.*

You might ask, 'Can't stories be created or made up?'

Of course they can, but not in this book and definitely not in the world of business.

'Can't I borrow from mythology?'

Of course you can if you have a huge memory bank for mythological stories and know how to connect them to business. But not in this book. In this book, and in the work I do, we will stick to stories being facts. After all, the currency of business is fact.

Given that this is a business book, a question that might be on your mind is what is the ROI of using stories? Fair question. And I have an answer. Actually two answers. One is €17 per word and the other is 28.06 times. I promise I didn't pull those numbers out of a hat.

In early 2016, the German *Huffington Post* reported a very interesting story about a young man who had an old 1997-manufactured Opel Tigra car. He wanted to sell it on eBay. His post was accompanied by a long story about his girlfriend being pregnant, his encounter with the police at eighteen, his relationship with his father and finally about his friend who advised him to sell the car to a hobby car enthusiast as it was neither new nor very good.

Compared to cars of the same vintage and use, which usually sell for around €2000, this auction finished at a whopping €55,750. It was a value addition of €53,000 because of a 3200-word story. As Susanna Gebauser, co-founder of the blog 'The Social Marketer', puts it, it was an ROI of almost €17 per word!

In the second case, in 2009, American authors Rob Walker and Joshua Glenn designed a curious experiment. They bought some cheap trinkets like corked bottles, birthday candles, paper fans, pencil cases, paperweights and napkin rings, etc., from thrift stores and garage sales. Then they asked some very creative writers to invent stories about them. They posted these stories and objects on eBay to see whether the invented stories enhanced the value of the objects. And they did. While they had bought the trinkets for $128, they sold them for $3612—an ROI of 2806 per cent or 28.06 times. This experiment was then repeated to raise money for charity which, not surprisingly, had a similar impact. These stories were not elaborate but were short and full of relatable emotions. I remember one about a tiny steel bottle opener with the Pabst Blue Ribbon logo embossed on it (an American Beer brand). The writer, Sean Howe, described his days when he was wooing Doona, a barmaid, the emotions he went through while sitting at the bar, watching her serving customers, returning their smiles, accepting tips and ever so often coming back to him to tell him about her dreams. He wrote about how he kept a watch over what he called the 'interlopers' while pretending that all he was doing was busy watching the liquor in the shelves. He then described a Thursday night when, after work, they took a few bottles to the stairs behind but she was already so drunk that she dropped this bottle opener through the slats and all they did was smoked and listened to the rain. This story got a buyer to bid $20.51 for an item bought for 25 cents. A 8200 per cent return on investment.

All the stories, the objects and the value addition are available on their site: www.significantobjects.com.

For some of my hard-nosed corporate readers, these stories may be too sentimental and cannot be representative of business situations. I disagree. Here are a few more data points that support my disagreement.

Jim Collins and Jerry Porras, in their book *Built to Last*,[2] talk about the increased financial results of companies who let their purpose drive what they do. How can you describe 'a powerful purpose'? I would say it is a story about the current and future of an organization that helps employees link the journey with their own motivation and inspires them to act on it. These companies are seen to outperform the general market 15:1 and comparison companies 6:1.

In a similar vein, two other writers John Kotter and James Heskett, in their book *Corporate Culture and Performance*,[3] said something similar. They shared that companies that have cultures based on their purpose and values outperform their peers who don't. They see a revenue growth which is four times faster and a share price growth that is twelve times faster. My favourite definition of culture is 'the way we do things here'. Purpose and values are not what is written in documents or put up on posters, it is the stories employees share of the company's and its employees' behaviour, and how they align with the present and the future planned for the organization.

I am sure these eye-popping returns on investment must have pre-empted any possible buyer's remorse you may have had about buying this book. I can also assure you that by the end of this book you would be convinced that devoting time to enhance your storytelling skills is one of the best investments you ever made.

But how do you lock your investment down?

Have you heard the story about Gillian Lynne? No? Here it is as narrated by Ken Robinson in his book *The Element*.[4]

Eight-year-old Gillian was not doing well in school. The fidgety girl underperformed in tests, had trouble writing legibly and continually missed assignment deadlines. She could also be a disruptive presence in class. Sometimes she would be so inattentive that it was as if she wasn't really there. She probably had a learning disorder and needed to change schools, moving to one that catered for kids with special needs. At least, this was the thinking that Gillian's current school outlined in a letter sent to her parents.

Gillian herself didn't understand what all the fuss was about. She was just a regular child, albeit a restless one. But her mother and father were anxious about her educational prospects. This happened in the 1930s, long before Attention Deficit Hyperactivity Disorder (ADHD) became a catchphrase to explain children's behavioural issues. There were also no options of medicating Gillian into obedience.

Instead, a psychological assessment seemed to be the best course of action. Upon entering the psychologist's intimidatingly formal oak-panelled office, Gillian fell into a big leather chair and tried not to squirm too much. The psychologist, who stared unnervingly at Gillian the whole time, questioned her mother at length. Eventually, the doctor came over to the girl and said that he and her mother needed to step outside for a few minutes. Before leaving, he turned on a radio that sat on his desk.

The psychologist took Gillian's mother into the corridor, where they both stood at a window that allowed them to look into the office discreetly. The doctor said they were just going to watch the girl for a few minutes. As the adults looked on, Gillian got up from the chair and started dancing gracefully around the room, moving in time to the music from the radio, a look of bliss lighting up her face. The psychologist turned to Gillian's mother and told her that there was nothing wrong with her daughter—she just wanted to dance.

He was right. When Gillian walked into her first dance class soon afterwards, she found herself surrounded by kindred spirits—people who, like her, loved being in motion. She worked hard in class and practised at home. She was eventually accepted into London's Royal Ballet School. Four decades later, after many successes as a performer and choreographer, she choreographed *Cats* and *The Phantom of the Opera*, two of the most successful musicals ever staged.

Had Gillian been deemed a problem child, she may never have found her calling. But because she was encouraged to be herself, she experienced a lifetime of joy.

Nice story, wouldn't you agree? If I asked you a few weeks from now whether you knew the story of Gillian Lynne, the choreographer of *Cats* and *The Phantom of the Opera*, you'd probably say yes. If I asked you a year later? Again most of you would probably say yes.

But imagine if in a meeting you wanted to stress on the importance of 'correct diagnosis', would Gillian's story pop up in your mind? Unlikely.

While we can easily recall stories when we are either told the title or reminded of the key character, we find it difficult to recall a story based on the lesson learnt or the moral. That's just how the human memory retrieval system works but that is not how we will try to retrieve stories when we want to use one in a business situation. Let's look at an example.

Suppose you are making a presentation tomorrow and want to make a point about how people shouldn't take their skills and competencies as a guarantee for success. You want to use a story to illustrate the point. Does a story come to you immediately? For most of you, it probably doesn't. But do you know the 'hare and tortoise' story? Of course you do. Isn't that a story about how skills and competencies do not guarantee success?

This story didn't pop into your head because your brain indexed it as per the characters, e.g., 'hare and tortoise' and the plot, e.g., 'the one in which the faster animal went to sleep and the slower animal continued and won the race'. You, however, were looking for it with the search string 'skills and competencies are not a guarantee for success'.

So how do you remember the right story when you need it?

I don't think I have been able to keep too many in my head, but the ones I have are there because I have done three things. First, I have paused to think and verbalize what message I get from the story. Second, I have tried to visualize the story in my head. And third, I have discussed the story and what it means with a friend or a colleague. While that works for a few stories, may be twenty or thirty, what about the hundreds of other stories I love and have used in presentations, speeches and discussions. For that, a 'process' needs to kick in—a process to catalogue stories and create an easy retrieval system, a system designed to retrieve stories using the business point we want to make rather than the characters or plot.

This is how it works. First, identify the key facts and critical elements of the story. For the story shared earlier they would be '1930', 'Gillian Lynne', 'fidgety', 'missed assignments', 'school said learning disorder', 'mother', 'psychologist', 'radio', 'dance', 'Royal Ballet School', 'Cats and The Phantom of the Opera'. I am sure you will all agree that even a decade later if I gave you just those seventeen words, you would be able to recall and retell, with a lot of details, the story. You may forget some elements like the 'oak-panelled office' of the psychologist or that the Royal Ballet School was in London. Neither of them are essential to the message of the story. You will remember more than enough to get your point across.

The next thing you need to do is create tags for the subjects for which you may use this story. Perhaps they will be 'the importance of a correct diagnosis', 'the importance of having people care for your future' or Ken Robinson's original thesis of 'finding your passion changes everything'. A great way to add tags is to tell the story to a few colleagues and ask what it means to them. Someone may say 'finding the right job for the right person'—after all, in 1930 the mother may have decided that the daughter need not go to any school. The interpretations that resonate with you are the tags you add.

Now, you need a notes application like Evernote that lets you tag notes. You need to create a new note. Use a labelling system that works for you. I love the way the episode titles of *Friends* say, 'The one where Joey moves out.' That way, during a search, the title itself will remind you of the story. Then put down in the body of the note the key elements. In the case of the above story, they would be the seventeen words we had identified—Gillian Lynne, fidgety, 1930, etc. Then, using the tagging option, key in the tags. The story is yours forever. We will discuss the storing and tagging process in detail in Chapter 3.

Years or months later, if you are preparing for a speech or a presentation and are looking for a story on the importance of a job fit, you can open the app and search the tag for 'right job, right person' and the Gillian Lynne story will pop up.

Yes, you will need to put in a little bit of effort to claim ownership of the stories you love. But the effort pays back many times over when you get recognized as an inspirational, engaging speaker who connects with the audience.

As you read books, hear anecdotes at work and fill your bag of stories, it will be nothing short of collecting gold dust. Mukul Deoras, who told me the wholesaler's story when making the point about learning from unexpected sources, today heads global marketing for one of the world's top FMCG companies—Colgate-Palmolive. He would surely agree that his ability to tell stories to make a point has been as useful as the science of alchemy is to a rookie magician!

So, as you start reading this book, I would urge you to make that effort and start storing the stories you read here and elsewhere. The habit will come in handy during your journey to storytelling stardom. Before continuing with the book, download Evernote and key in Gillian's story as a starting point. While doing this now will not guarantee that you will create a large repository, not doing it now will surely reduce the probability of doing it later. Go ahead, put the book down and start the story bank.

This book has been written with the very specific objective of helping you become a business storyteller. While it will cover the background and fundamentals of business storytelling, it will also give you the tools, techniques and processes by which you can coach yourself to powerfully use stories in business.

Stories at Work is divided into three parts. Chapters 1 to 4 cover the fundamentals and set the stage for the introduction to various patterns of stories that can be used in business. These patterns are detailed in chapters 5 to 9. In chapters 10 to 15, we bring it all together and look at how various elements of stories combine to address business challenges like embedding values, managing change, managing knowledge, supercharging the sales pitch, making impactful presentations and storytelling with data. We then cover ethics and storytelling and finally finish with how you can create a storytelling organization.

Go ahead and spin the wheel, and as the wheel turns, be sure to collect as much gold dust as you can.

PART I

Foundation

Stories Are Powerful—Evolution and Biology Have a Role to Play

FOR SALE: BABY shoes. Never worn.

When you read these six words, what feelings do they evoke? Don't these six words immediately make us empathize with an unknown, grief-stricken woman? We can almost visualize the situation and our hearts go out to her.

Ernest Hemingway wrote this story, calling it a six-word novel. It shows the almost visceral effect stories can have on us. But why does it happen?

In the introduction, I discussed how a chemical called oxytocin is released in the brain when we hear and 'experience' stories. Paul Zak's team's tests showed that oxytocin is the same chemical that is produced in our brains when we are trusted and that it motivates cooperation. This enhances the sense of empathy. So, it was no wonder that when stories were told prior to asking for charitable donations, listeners were more inclined to contribute.

Now, let's delve a little deeper into the relationship between our brains and stories.

Over the last few decades there has been a gigantic leap in our understanding of how our brains react to stories. Some fascinating work has been done in the areas of cognitive science, neurological science, evolutionary biology, development psychology and neural net modelling.

A brilliant book on this subject is *Story Proof: The Science behind the Startling Power of Story* by Kendall Haven.[1] He pored over 350 books, seventy articles and over 1500 studies covering over 1,00,000 pages to understand how the human mind receives, processes and responds to stories. Every study he describes in the book is fascinating.

From this book, and from several others that I have read on the brain and stories, I want to share six studies that are profoundly relevant:

1. Evolutionary predisposition
2. Childhood story exposure
3. Chemical Post-it notes
4. Neural coupling
5. Monkey see, monkey do, monkey feel
6. Data brain, story brain

Evolutionary Predisposition

Humans have been telling stories for over 1,00,000 years. Evolutionary biologists confirm that this has rewired the human brain to be predisposed to think in story terms and explain things in story structures. This has also resulted in our love for stories.

Here is a little experiment you can do to see how wired we are for stories. Have you ever been part of a meeting with a roomful of people who found their mobile screens more interesting than the discussion? Sure you have. The next time this happens, find the right opportunity and say something like 'I remember six years ago . . .' and stop. Observe what happens. Almost every head will rise and look at you. It is almost as if a town crier screams inside everyone's brain 'Look out! There may be a story coming.'

The proof of our predisposition to stories is apparent from the time we are born. As Haven reports, many researchers have studied the reaction and mental processes of babies and found that humans think in story terms since birth. In a seminal book on this subject, *Acts of Meaning*, psychologist Jerome Bruner[2] reports on long years of clinical studies that have shown that we are born preprogrammed to search for, and to create meaning from, story elements. All of you who have had children would definitely attest to that fact. Think back to what your child was able to do once he was able to string words together into a sentence. If you walked in and saw him looking guiltily at a broken vase and asked 'how did this happen?', did he say 'I was running and hit the table and the vase fell and broke?' Or did he say 'Spiderman was fighting with the bad guys and during the fight the vase fell and broke?' Chances are very high that if the child was as naughty as I was, he would have said the latter. Did you teach him how to craft stories? No. You had to teach him language, spelling, handwriting and mathematics but not how to tell stories.

Scientists who study the human brain have been able to observe, at an incredibly detailed level, how we think. Using thousands of electrodes, they can now monitor every single brain cell and observe how it responds to external inputs like pictures and sounds. This ability has allowed them to study how our brains react to incoming information.

In his second book on storytelling, *Story Smart: Using the Science of Story to Persuade, Influence, Inspire, and Teach,* Kendall Haven[3] reports on something truly amazing. Putting together inputs from four different sources[4] he concludes that 'the brain converts raw experience into story form and then considers, ponders, remembers and acts on the self-created story, not the actual input experience!' That is a fascinating conclusion. This means that even when our brain receives input in the form of data, information, logic or analysis, it doesn't directly work on them. The brain first creates a story with them and then processes this story.

This also seems to indicate that when we send our information already packaged in a story structure it doesn't get altered too much.

Another evolutionary predisposition comes from our survival instinct. During the hunter-gatherer days, if we saw a partial shape of what appeared to be a tiger, our brain would fill in the missing information, perceive it as a tiger and prepare for action—fight or flight. This would happen even if it did not turn out to be a tiger later.

That hasn't changed even now. If while passing a shady neighbourhood alone we see some people approaching with sticks in their hand, we don't stop to ask them their intent. Instead, we turn around and find an alternative way home.

This predisposition to filling in the blanks also works when bits and pieces of information are abstract and don't make sense. The brain doesn't instruct us to seek new information. It does some pattern recognition and simply fills up gaps from previous experience. This perhaps explains why many a time your team members seem to give you vigorous nods of understanding. However, when you ask them what they understood, they say something completely different.

Childhood Story Exposure

As parents, we have observed that explaining the workings of the world to children works better when we use stories and story structures. Cultures across the world have, since time immemorial, been using bedtime stories not only to put their children to sleep but also to drive home key messages—values, behaviour and knowledge. The more a child, in the formative years, engages their story neural net to interpret incoming sensory input, the more likely they are to do it as adults in the future.

When we reflect on some of the best teachers we have had growing up, we will recall that all of them were great storytellers.

Deep exposure to stories through the key years of brain development results in adults who are irrevocably hardwired to think in story terms.

Chemical Post-it Notes

Here is a question for readers from India. Do you remember exactly where you were on the night of 26/11? That was when the Taj and Oberoi hotels were under siege. Do you remember which city you were in? Which house were you in? Which room were you in when the news reached you? It would be very unlikely that you don't.

Why does this happen?

In his book *Brain Rules*, molecular biologist John Medina[5] explains: 'When the brain detects an emotionally charged event, the amygdala releases dopamine into the system. Because dopamine greatly aids memory and information processing, you could say it creates a Post-it note that reads, "Remember this."' The brain placing a chemical Post-it note on a given piece of information means that the information is going to be robustly processed. This is quite evident with the 26/11 example. It is vividly remembered even after almost a decade.

Neural Coupling

In a room in Uri Hasson's lab in Princeton, five people are lying in the dark. Their brains are under continuous scanning using functional Magnetic Resonance Imaging (fMRI) scanners. The scanners are recording brain patterns, and all five are different. In another part of the same dark room is Jim O'Grady, a very talented storyteller. His brain, too, is being scanned.

Jim starts telling a story. 'So, I am banging out my story and I know it's good, then I start to make it better . . .' As his voice trails off, one can hear laughter from the five listeners. Jim continues.

A strange thing starts happening. The brain pattern of all the five listeners begins to synchronize and lock on to Jim's brain pattern. This phenomenon is called 'neural entrainment' or speaker–listener neural coupling. Further experiments prove that this coupling stops as soon as the speaker stops communicating. Uri then tried another experiment. He played backwards a recording of Jim telling this story. This ensured that while the tone and tenor of the voice remained the same, the sound produced had no meaning. No coupling happened in this case. An edit of the audio was also made by putting together random words from Jim's story recording. This was played to the participants. No coupling.

So, clearly, when a story is told and it has meaning, the brain patterns synch. Another interesting phenomenon was observed during this experiment. There are times when the listener's brain pattern goes ahead of the tellers. The listener is anticipating what will come next. After the experiment, the story comprehension of the participants shows that greater the anticipatory behaviour, greater the understanding.[6]

What a dramatic demonstration of the ability of stories to allow a listener to comprehend what the teller is saying!

Monkey See, Monkey Do, Monkey Feel

In the early 1990s, Dr Vittorio Gallese and two of his colleagues from the University of Parma made an accidental but quite remarkable neuro-scientific discovery.[7]

They had set out to study the neurons responsible for motor activities in macaque monkeys. By planting electrodes in a monkey's brain, they could observe which areas of the brain were activated while the monkey performed various actions—such as grabbing a nut.

One day, as one of the researchers reached out for his lunch, he noticed something odd on one of the monkey's monitors. The ventral premotor cortex—or the area that would normally react to the monkey grabbing food—lit up. But the monkey wasn't reaching out for food, he was just observing the researcher grab his own lunch.

The same neurons in the monkey's brain that fired up when it performed an action also fired up when it saw someone else perform the same action.

Going forward, Dr Gallese studied and confirmed that 'mirror neurons' are involved in the most basic human abilities: learning, communicating, empathy and even language.

Studies have also shown that mirror neurons fire up even when we read or hear words that describe the same action. So whether we do the action, see the action being done or hear of it, the same neurons light up. This leads us to feel the same way when we hear of an action as when we do the same action.

So when someone describes a pain they went through, we feel the same way. For example, when someone tells a sad story, we feel sad. When someone tells a horror story, we feel scared. This feeling leads to empathy.

As we saw earlier with the 26/11 Mumbai terror attack example, when we experience something and have an emotion about the same, we remember the incident.

When the storyteller tells us a story, the same neurons are fired up in the minds of both the listener and the storyteller. That is why they are called mirror neurons. This is a major reason why stories often become as memorable as our own experiences.

This, of course, has an adverse effect as well called 'invented memory'. We'll discuss how to navigate around that in Chapter 5.

Data Brain, Story Brain

Why do we feel so much more engaged when we hear a narrative about events as opposed to listening to data about the same?

Brain studies can explain this. When we listen to or see a PowerPoint presentation with boring bullet points, certain parts of the brain are activated. Scientists call these Broca's area and Wernicke's area. Overall, bullet points on the PowerPoint screen light up the language-processing parts in our brain. There we decode words into meaning. Nothing happens beyond that in the brain.

When we are told a story on the other hand, things change dramatically. Not only are the language-processing parts in our brain activated, but other areas too get activated. How does that work?

In a 2006 study published in the journal *NeuroImage*,[8] researchers from Spain noticed that if someone tells us about how delicious certain foods are, our sensory cortex lights up. If it's about motion, our motor cortex becomes active.

Stories impact more areas of the brain than data does and hence stories involve us much more. This increases the likelihood of us taking action when we hear stories and not just data.

Imagine you are making a presentation on road safety. In it, you include the following observations:

1. Every hour, sixteen lives are lost to road crashes in India.
2. Though we have just 1 per cent of the world's vehicles, India accounts for over 10 per cent of global road crash fatalities.
3. Studies have shown that one in four crashes happen due to distractions created by texting and speaking on the phone while driving.

When listening to this and decoding the words, the standard language-processing regions of the listener's brain are activated. Now think of whether listening to this serious and startling piece of data would change the behaviour among listeners.

Now imagine a different scenario. This time you share this story.

Ravi was in tears when narrating why he gets so agitated when he sees people using their cellphones while driving.

He recalls his daughter Maya's first day as a university student. She was busy planning what to wear and how to do her hair. She was full of enthusiasm. She couldn't wait to see some old friends and make new ones. Before she left the house, they shared an ordinary breakfast—some poha and a cup of tea. Nothing extravagant. Yet, Ravi will never forget that simple meal. It's locked in his memory along with the radiant smile on Maya's face as she went out of the door. She never made it to the university. She began texting a friend while driving, and being distracted did not notice a vehicle driving on the wrong side of the road. She crashed into it. That small action changed everything.

After sharing this story, you share the data on road accidents. For example, sixteen lives lost every hour, 10 per cent of crash fatalities with 1 per cent of vehicles, one in four crashes due to mobile phones, etc.

What happened as you told the story? Everything I spoke of earlier would have started happening. Speaker–listener neural coupling would have aligned your audiences' brain pattern to yours. Mirror neurons would have made you and your audience feel what Ravi felt. Chemicals like oxytocin would have been released and that, along with the mirror neurons, would have created empathy. Dopamine would have been released in order to create a Post-it note in your listener's brain to ensure that the memory sticks.

Can you imagine how much more powerful this is than simply sharing data?

The story tendency in the brain is a good thing. As Haven says in his book *Story Proof*, 'Story is emerging as the interstate express carpool lane into the mind. Why? Just as traffic engineers designed those special lanes to speed traffic into major cities, so too, evolution and the brain's experience during its plastic years have engineered story pathways as express routes into the human mind.'

In this world of increasing noise and clutter, an ability to find an 'expressway' to the listeners' minds can be the most powerful skill in a leader's repertoire.

2

Why Stories?

A FEW YEARS after I started StoryWorks, I bumped into Shankar Lakhotia at an airport. Shankar and I had worked together in 1996 when I was setting up the sales and distribution system for the newly created Nepal Lever Limited. We had last seen each other in 2002 and quickly exchanged notes about our lives in the last fourteen years. After I told Shankar about the work I do with business storytelling, he said, 'I am not surprised. You were quite a storyteller even when I first met you twenty years ago.' The statement surprised me as I didn't consciously cultivate the art and science of storytelling. I asked him whether he remembered any examples. He said, 'I do. How can I ever forget the story you told us to explain competitive advantage.' He went on to narrate it.

Two CEOs had gone on a little fishing trip. After they caught a fish, they lit a small fire using dried driftwood to barbecue it. The smell of the grilled fish attracted a giant grizzly bear. One of the CEOs panicked and screamed, 'What are we going to do?'

The other CEO calmly opened his backpack and took out his running shoes. His fishing partner looked at him and asked with a lot of sarcasm, 'Do you seriously think you can outrun a grizzly?' The other CEO replied, 'I don't have to outrun the bear. I just have to outrun you.'

The shoes were his competitive advantage.

That story is now clichéd but was not so well known twenty years ago. While I surely wouldn't use that story now, Shankar's recollection was a reinforcement of my belief. I always knew that stories were memorable and impactful. But to experience it first-hand from somebody, to whom I had narrated the story twenty years ago, was another thing altogether.

A major reason we use stories to convey a message is that they are memorable. They help us remember a point that's being made or a lesson that needs to be learnt. This has been proven time and again.

Jean Mandler, author of *Stories, Scripts and Scenes: Aspects of Schema Theory*,[1] has conducted several experiments with children and adults, which show that when experiences are not framed into a story, they suffer memory loss. In one such experiment, she presented two sets of participants with a combination of images. For one set, the images were randomly arranged (e.g., pictures of two three-storeyed houses, a plane, two cars and a palm tree). The other set was arranged to resemble a 'real world' scene (e.g., two houses side by side, one car parked behind another in the space in front of the houses, the palm tree off on one side and a plane over the houses). There was a spatial relationship between the objects. In other words, the mind could create a story. A week later, the participants who were shown the arranged images recalled the images better than those who were shown the same images in a random order.

Here is another example of how powerful story and visualization can be. How many of you have used the chanting method to memorize a shopping list? I have used it often, repeatedly muttering to myself, 'egg, bread, olive oil, mustard, ginger, banana', on my way to the grocery store. Then, I learnt the story technique which requires one to take a random list of words and create a story around these, visualizing it in the process.

Imagine if the words were: river, bicycle, Barbie doll, cigarette and noodles. What are the chances that you would remember this list by the time you finished reading this chapter? Very low. Now, here is a story.

> One day, a teacher was riding his bicycle along the banks of a river. He had in his hand a Barbie doll that he had bought for his daughter. As he was riding, he saw a nun smoking a cigarette. The nun waved to him. He stopped in front of her and got down from the bicycle, still clutching on to the Barbie Doll. They sat down by the river and shared the noodles he was carrying in the tiffin box that he had clamped to the carrier of his bicycle.

This is a surreal situation and an awful story, but can you get the visuals out of your head? Let's revisit this at the end of the chapter.

Apart from stories being memorable, there are many other reasons why they can be powerful in business. Some of them are:

1. Stories help explain critical, complex messages.
2. Stories are credible.
3. Stories induce 'lean-in' behaviour.
4. Stories inspire action.
5. Stories spread.

Stories Help Explain Critical Complex Messages

What is the point of being smart if nobody understands what you have to say? And no, I am not asking you to dumb down your message. Complex ideas are complex for a reason. Dumbing down the message reduces it to something trivial that can easily be dismissed. Often, the complexity of the message is caused not by the complexity of the idea but by the big abstract words we use and the lack of structure in communication.

First, let's look at abstraction. MBAs, like me, are famous for their barely contained lust for business jargon. I think a lot of it starts at the institute when we solve cases where we are asked at the end: 'If you were the CEO, what would you do?' Surely that required a 'deep dive' and a 'cross-pollination' of ideas before some 'blue sky thinking' could identify the 'elephant in the room'. Phew!

Fresh MBA-holders are not alone. Recently, Lucy Kellaway of the *Financial Times* took the *McKinsey Quarterly* to task for similar language. 'With more discontinuity and volatility, with long-term charts no longer looking like smooth upward curves, long-held assumptions giving way and seemingly powerful business models becoming upended' is an actual line from an article in the *McKinsey Quarterly*.

If you are one of those people who are now sick of 'boiling the ocean', 'taking it offline' or 'going after the low-hanging fruit', you must refer your colleagues or bosses to a new research in the *Personality and Social Psychology Bulletin*. The study, conducted by New York University and a Swiss university, shows very powerfully that when you want to come across as believable and trustworthy, using concrete language is the way to go. In these experiments, the professors found that statements written in a definitive manner were more likely to be judged as true than when the same statements were written using fuzzy language. The study found that using verbs like 'count' and 'write' were solid, concrete and unambiguous, while 'help' and 'insult' are open to interpretation.

But if 'help' and 'insult' are ambiguous, where does that leave 'cascade' and 'onboarding', asks Jena McGregor in the *Washington Post*. This problem becomes bigger when younger, less-experienced managers believe that simple language makes a person sound less credible. Many people think that they have to use complex corporate language to impress people. My learning with storytelling finally freed me from talking in incomprehensible corporate jargon and empowered me to communicate simply, directly and efficiently.

Articulation of important messages like strategy brings two other adversaries—co-creation and wordsmithing—face-to-face. We start with something that might sound fairly robust and straightforward. Then, we call in colleagues and teammates and sometimes a bunch of consultants for their inputs, after which we look for powerful words. A humorous but hard-hitting YouTube video by Dan Heath on why most mission statements are so terrible is very accurate.

The video starts with an inspiring 'Our mission is to serve the tastiest damn pizza in Wake county.' It is collaboration, co-creation and wordsmithing that gives us this work of art: 'Our mission is to present with integrity the highest quality entertainment solution to families.' Sounds unbelievable, but the steps from one to the other and the logic behind them are no different from many that I have personally heard.

I have seen many leaders finding it very difficult to use plain language, especially when it comes to communicating something like strategy. With storytelling skills learnt and honed, this no longer remains an uphill struggle.

Now for the second problem: the lack of structure. It is important to understand the difference between the oral word and the written word. I have always believed that I am a very clear communicator because no one has ever come back after reading my emails or proposals and said that they don't understand. But that may just be because if ever they got lost in my written document and did not understand something because of my lack of structure, they could always go back a few paragraphs and see if it made sense. Unfortunately, when we speak, we don't have a pause and rewind button, and when the listener loses understanding at any point, it is game over.

That's where oral storytelling becomes very powerful. We are never complex or abstract in our language when we tell stories and hence 'I need some face time with you. Can you ring-fence a slot in your schedule?' is quickly replaced with 'We need to meet.' A story forces us to have a structure in order to be meaningful. We will talk more about a very easy way to cast our messages into a story structure in Chapter 7: Getting Strategies to Stick.

Stories Are Credible

Imagine this. You work in an industry where an aggressive entrant has dramatically reduced profitability among all incumbents. This has resulted in pressure on costs and almost all companies have already had a huge round of retrenchments resulting in extensive job losses. Most employees feel that this is just the beginning and further downsizing will soon happen. To make it worse, a large number of employees, having spent most of their time in this industry, feel that they are virtually unemployable elsewhere. In the middle of this uncertain and chaotic environment, two of the largest companies announce a merger. It seems certain that once the merger is complete, almost half the managers will become redundant due to duplication of roles. This increases the uncertainty and rumours, causing distractions and impacting day-to-day operations. The human resource department has been working overtime to relay messages about how every employee will be accommodated either in their current jobs or retrained for other roles. But this hasn't done much to alleviate the anxiety.

In this situation, your CEO calls for an 'all hands' meeting. A mega town hall has been organized and this is what the CEO says:

I have been getting continuous feedback that many of you are worried about job losses due to redundancies the merger might create. That is completely unwarranted. The purpose of me talking to you today is to assure you that this won't happen. You can take my word for it. This won't happen because we are the better company and when people are chosen you will always be seen as the better person for the role. We will also expand aggressively and this will mean that we will need all the talent we can get. It's time everyone stopped talking about redundancies and started focusing on what they can do to help build the business. You have my personal guarantee that all our leaders will fight for you. Continuing to talk about redundancies only gets in the way of what we need to focus on. For the good of the business, we need to focus on growth and retaining market share. I ask you all to support me in this.

Take a moment to think about how much the CEO's speech has reassured you and your colleagues. On a scale of 0 to 10, assign a score of how reassured you are, 10 being completely reassured.

Now imagine another scenario. Instead of the speech above, the CEO says this:

I know that many of you are concerned that there will be huge job losses due to the merger. I understand the anxiety given the pressure on costs and the previous round of layoffs. Two weeks ago, at the management committee meeting in Delhi, Harish, our operations director, presented a plan on geographical expansion. We have all agreed on this.

Starting this month, we will be entering two new markets and that will go up to eight new markets over the next few months. By the end of the year, we will actually need more people than we currently have. While the expansion will not happen in one go, we have decided to not lose the fabulous talent we have in the short term. Ravi, our CFO, has agreed and built the cost into the annual business plan. The joint board of the two companies approved this plan yesterday. So, while the bitter experience of losing some of your colleagues a while back and the news of the imminent merger has made you worry about further redundancies, I wanted to put your minds at rest on this issue and request you to focus on the critical task of ensuring that we continue to grow and not lose our share of the market.

Which version of the speech would have assured your colleagues and you more? Again assign a score between 0 and 10 on how reassured you feel. I am assuming the second version scored way above the first. Right? That is because the first one is full of assertions. And assertions aren't always credible. The second one has a story about the management committee and a joint board meeting, making the message more credible. We will have a better understanding of how to build credibility in Chapter 5: Using Stories to Build Rapport and Credibility.

Stories Induce a 'Lean-in' Behaviour

It is said that a picture is worth a thousand words. I have over 350 photographs of participants in my workshops telling stories to their table groups. A table group usually includes four participants. The photographs are taken during the first exercise, where the participants are asked to narrate an anecdote from their life. Other than the animation on the speakers' faces and their gestures, the one thing common in all the pictures is that all the listeners lean in.

Now think of every meeting you go to or all the presentations you ever sat through. Think of the postures of most of the people in the room. Were they leaning in or leaning back?

However, if any presenter starts narrating a story, most people engage and lean in.

Stories Inspire Action

No, I am not talking about stories of Mahatma Gandhi, Nelson Mandela or that charismatic founder or CEO inspiring people to follow a certain path. Though their stories did inspire others to act, I am talking about a completely different kind of stories. I am talking about getting people to act, and act quickly, in day-to-day business situations.

> It was a village woman named Sufiya Begum who taught me the true nature of poverty in Bangladesh. Like many village women, Sufiya lived with her husband and small children in a crumbling mud hut with a leaky thatched roof. To provide food for her family, Sufiya worked all day in her muddy yard making bamboo stools. Yet somehow her hard work was unable to lift her family out of poverty. I wondered why?

With these words, Muhammad Yunus, the founder of Bangladesh's Grameen Bank, the pioneer of the microcredit movement and a Nobel Prize winner, starts his narrative about the people he helped.

He goes on to talk about how Sufiya relied on local moneylenders for the cash she needed to buy bamboo for the stools she sold. These moneylenders would charge an astronomical interest rate—anywhere between 10 per cent a week to 10 per cent a day!

When Muhammad Yunus probed further, he found that Sufiya was not alone. In a single village called Jobra he found forty-two people who had borrowed a total of 856 taka—an amount less than $27 at that time. He immediately offered $27 to them and got rid of their debt.

The joy and relief his beneficiaries experienced made him want to do more. He ended his story with 'that has been my mission ever since.'

When, after telling this story, he asked his listeners to help bring affordable credit to every poor person in the world, he almost always received a flood of pledges.[2]

Most people I know in business would have been more comfortable making a PowerPoint presentation with lots of facts and figures, like the per capita debt of people in rural Bangladesh and compare that with the figures of Asia and the world. The really erudite ones would have introduced Amartya Sen's theory of absolute and relative poverty, combining it with data of countries or communities where reduction or removal of debt has led to alleviation of poverty. A data-led approach like that would rarely trigger action. However, if you bring data and story together, the result is bound to be more encouraging.

Let me share a hypothetical scenario. Imagine I am the head of organizational health and safety of a giant cement manufacturing firm that has been struggling with its safety record for several years. Last year was no better. Now, imagine that you are a part of the management committee of this organization and I am presenting my plan for 2018. I start with a table that compares the data for 2017 with 2016.

	2016	2017	% -/+
FATALITIES	6	8	+33%
NON-FATALITIES (Major)	14	12	-14%
NON-FATALITIES (Minor)	37	43	+16%
NEAR MISSES	120	170	+42%

I then say, 'As you can see we have had a 33 per cent increase in fatalities, minor accidents and near misses have gone up significantly. While major accidents that included loss of limbs have gone down by 14 per cent, the absolute number is still in double digits. Despite a lot of initiatives, these numbers haven't changed and being so much behind the Indian industry average is unacceptable. My search for a solution has led me to a boutique consultancy in Paris which has worked with several industries, including our own, to dramatically improve their safety record. They have agreed to work with us and have committed that over a twelve-month period, they will be able to bring these numbers down. Not just below Indian but worldwide industry averages. My request to you, the members of the management committee, is to sanction Rs 2 crore for this consulting project.'

I would like you to pause a bit and think about your response. Would you say go ahead, would you say no arguing that this is an in-house responsibility, or would you ask for more analysis? Would you ask me to come back to the next month's management committee meeting with more data such as 'investigate further the causes, isolate whether these numbers have a geographical skew, are these accidents happening more in the night shift compared to the day shift, etc.?' I hope you have made a decision.

Now, try to erase the previous scenario from your mind. Let us start all over again. This time I walk in and put up a slide that has the picture of a lower-income Indian household with three young women and an elderly lady staring forlornly at a garlanded portrait of a middle-aged man. I start by saying, 'I met Ramesh Menon's family two months ago. As you know, we lost Ramesh in the boiler accident in Jabalpur last year. While we have announced an ex-gratia payment of Rs 5 lakh, his wife was very worried about how she would get her three daughters educated and married.'

I then put up a picture of a person in a hospital with his right arm bandaged and a steel rod jutting out. I go on to say, 'Last week, I met Vivek Sahay. Vivek lost his right arm in the unfortunate mixer explosion in Jalna last month. We have committed lifetime employment to Vivek, but he knows that he can never get the kind of jobs he could have got if he still had his right arm.' I then put up the same table you saw and continue, 'Ramesh and Vivek are not alone. We lost eight Rameshs last year, a 33 per cent increase. While the major limb loss accidents reduced by 14 per cent, they still accounted for twelve Viveks. The huge number of minor accidents and near misses are nothing but Rameshs and Viveks waiting to happen. We cannot let this continue! As you are aware, we have tried many initiatives but none of them have worked. In my search for a solution I found a boutique consultancy in Paris which has worked with several industries, including our own. They have helped to dramatically improve their safety record. They have agreed to work with us and have committed that over a twelve-month period they will be able to bring these numbers down, not just below Indian but worldwide industry averages. For this project, I would request you to approve Rs 2 crore.'

I again want you to pause and ask yourself what your reaction, as a management committee member, might be. Would it be the same as after the previous speech? I think not.

Even if you decided that you would like some further analysis, would you be comfortable to wait till the next management committee meeting a month later? Or would you say, 'This is an extremely critical issue. When is the soonest that we can have more data?' Obviously, a story inspires action which data alone cannot.

The question is: Did I lie? Did I do something unprofessional? Did I emotionally blackmail you? The answer to all three questions is no. What I did was put the data in context. As I mentioned in a previous chapter, my definition of stories in business is that *a story is a fact wrapped in context and delivered with emotion*. And that is exactly what I did in the situation described earlier.

It's quite simple. If we listen to a PowerPoint presentation with a lot of data and boring bullet points, certain parts in the brain—Broca's area and Wernicke's area—get activated. Overall, it hits the language-processing parts in our brains, where we decode words into meaning. And that's it, nothing else happens.

When we are told a story, things change dramatically. Not only are the language-processing parts in our brains activated, but other important areas are as well. For example, the area in the brain that would have got activated had the listener actually met these victims also got activated. If you hear the words 'perfume' or 'coffee', the olfactory cortex lights up. When we hear metaphors like: 'The singer had a velvet voice', or 'He had leathery hands', the sensory cortex lights up.

So, the story about Ramesh and Vivek gets the listener to experience the same emotions that the teller would have gone through when he met their families. That, when coupled with the overall safety data of the company, gets the whole brain of the listener engaged in the decision.

When we hear a story that involves us emotionally or see a movie that engages us in a way that we feel empathy towards one of the characters, we are experiencing what persuasion research calls 'narrative transportation'. Stories that involve us emotionally are the ones that move us to action.

Stories Spread

21 September 1995.

Just before dawn, a worshipper at a temple in south Delhi was doing what he had done for years. He was making a symbolic offering of milk to the statue of Lord Ganesh. But this day was different. Unlike other days, when the gesture was indeed symbolic, on this day, the spoonful of milk held up to the statue was seen to disappear. It was as if the idol had consumed the milk. Word of this mind-boggling phenomenon spread like wildfire. By mid-morning, radio and TV channels were reporting about Ganesh idols from all corners of the country drinking the milk being offered to them. By noon, the news had spread well beyond India with temples in the UK, Canada, the UAE and Nepal substantiating the claim. Milk sales shot up across the country with New Delhi reporting a 30 per cent jump.

I remember looking with disbelief at how hundreds of managers, many with engineering and business management degrees from the best institutes in India, were lining outside temples to participate in this miracle. I remember thinking how the sales of the product I was handling could meet its ten-year target in a day if I could replicate a similar situation. No surprises here that a good story will always go viral, causing the ripples to spread far and wide.

So, here are some questions for you. How powerful would it be if every time you spoke people believed you? Every time you spoke people leaned in to listen? Every time you spoke people remembered what you said? Every time you spoke people were inspired to take action? Every time you spoke people went ahead and spread your message?

How powerful would that be?

That is the power that business storytelling can get you. That is the power I have helped hundreds of corporate leaders across functions and industries build. And that is the power you can harness by understanding the processes, structures and the science that follows in the rest of this book.

Now, before you go on, try and recall the seven words we were trying to remember using the story of the teacher and the nun. How many do you recall? (The words are reproduced on the next page).

River
Bicycle
Barbie Doll
Cigar
Pasta

3

How to Build Your Story Bank

Two monks were walking from their monastery to another one nearby. One was an old wise monk and the other was a novice, an apprentice monk.

As they walked in silence, they came across a river. Unseasonal rains had caused the river to run high. On the banks of the river was a young lady in a kimono, not sure whether it was safe for her to cross. When she saw the two monks, she looked relived and asked for help.

The young monk was aghast. He exclaimed, 'Don't you see that I am a monk? I took a vow of chastity.'

'I require nothing from you that could impede your vow, but simply a little help to cross the river,' the young woman replied with a smile.

'I will not . . . I can . . . do nothing for you,' said the embarrassed young monk.

At this point, the elderly monk stepped forward and said, 'Climb on to my back and I'll help you cross.'

Upon reaching the other side, the old monk put the lady down. She thanked him and he responded with a 'welcome'. With that, he started walking towards his destination.

The young apprentice was agitated. 'How could you do this? This is against our order. You are supposed to be my mentor. You are supposed to show me the way. When we return, I am going to ask them to change my mentor.'

The young monk went on and on till they reached the next monastery.

On reaching the gate, the old monk paused, looked at the young monk and said, 'I did carry the lady, but I put her down on the banks of the river. It seems like you are still carrying her.'

This is a beautiful parable that can be used in many business situations to make a point about carrying baggage and losing perspective, or about letting go of the past, or about confusing between the letter and spirit of the law.

A year from now, if I asked any of you whether you knew the 'two monks' story, I am certain you will all answer in the affirmative. That is because stories stick.

However, say a few weeks from now, if you were looking for a story to use in your office to make a point about confusing between the letter and spirit of the law, it is highly likely that many of you would not remember this story.

You may recollect that in the introductory chapter we discussed a process of cataloguing stories. We also discussed a retrieval system that allows us to find the stories from our database using the business point we want to make, a system that should throw up 'two monks' when we look for stories about the confusion between the letter and spirit of the law.

Since the creation of such a story bank is so vital, I am going to revise the process using this story. I hope you have downloaded Evernote and already stored the Gillian Lynne story.

Let's start. First, we label the story. In my story bank, I have labelled it 'Two Monks and the Baggage'. This is what Evernote calls the 'Note Title'.

Then, in the body of the note, we put down the key elements of the story. In this case, they would be 'two monks', 'river crossing', 'woman', 'carry on the back', 'you are still carrying her'. I am sure you will all agree that even a decade later if I gave you those five elements, just fourteen words, you would be able to recall and retell the story with a fair amount of accuracy. You may forget some elements like unseasonal rain or the fact that the woman was wearing a kimono. Neither are essential to the message of the story. You will remember more than enough to get your point across.

The next thing you need to do is create tags of the various business points you think you might illustrate using this story. Perhaps they will be 'putting down baggage', 'letting go of the past' and 'letter and spirit of the law'. A great way to add tags is to tell the story to a few colleagues and ask what it meant to them. Someone may say 'removing biases' or 'missing the ability to observe because you are stuck on an idea', after all the young monk did not enjoy the journey in the beautiful location. Whichever interpretations resonate with you are the tags you add. The story is now yours forever.

Someday, when you are preparing for a speech or a presentation and looking for a story on say 'the difference between letter and spirit of the law', the 'two monks' story will open once you open your app and search for the tag 'letter and spirit'.

Yes, you need to make this little effort to create ownership of the stories you love. But the effort pays back many times over in the form of being recognized as an inspirational, engaging speaker who connects with the audience.

Now, as you go through this book, use this process to store stories that resonate with you. As you make it a habit, your collection will grow and so will your reputation as a storyteller.

I will add a caution here. Not everything that is labelled a story is a story.

Let's take this excerpt from a website. It appeared under the heading 'Our Story'. I have changed certain elements to not embarrass the people in that company who put together the website.

In 1775, our founder, John Doe, invested in this country and started, what is today, the nation's longest-running financial institution. You could say, 'The buck started here.' In the 230 years since then, countries have been created. Borders have been erased. And new markets have emerged. But the essential things remain constant. We've endured by continually looking to the future and staying invested in innovation. We created the first <this>, the first

<that>, and the first <and the other>. Today, we're the investment management and investment services company that oversees $32.2 trillion. And we've become one of the world's top ten investment managers. We help clients conduct business in thirty-five countries and 100 markets, which gives us a unique vantage point to see the world like no one else. We're <The Big Financial Institution>. And we're the investment company for the world.

Is that a story? Certainly not. It is a list of assertions. The other common mistake is labelling a sequence of events or a timeline as a story. Here is another real, but masked, example.

We were founded in 1890 during India's Swadeshi (Freedom) movement. After failing in several ventures, we started making widget A and in 1915 we made India's first item B, in 1920 our products were endorsed by senior members of the freedom movement, in 1925 we entered a new industry C, in 1945 we set up an industrial township . . . so on and so forth till 2016.

This too is not a story.

Then what is a story? The definition I follow was put together by Shawn Callahan and Mark Schenk, who, as I mentioned earlier, run one of the world's leading business storytelling companies. According to them, there are five elements that are essential ingredients for a story.

1. Stories usually start in one of the two ways: with a time marker or a place marker. Most oral stories start with time

markers. So if you hear some say 'On Tuesday . . .' or 'A few months ago . . .' or 'In 1992 . . .' there is a good chance that you will hear a story.

2. Stories are always about something happening—a causal sequence of events. This event followed this event which resulted in that event. Good stories help you see what's happening. Great stories help you feel what's happening.

3. If you hear people's names, and in particular if you hear dialogues, you know you are hearing a story.

4. It isn't a story unless something unanticipated happens. A story is a promise to the listener that they will learn something new. It has to contain something that is at least a little unexpected.

5. While I often like to leave the story at this stage and let the listener draw the obvious conclusion, sometimes people are more comfortable in making sure the message is clear and driven home, and for that the fifth element is:

6. A relevance statement. Why am I telling you this story? What is the business point you are making? The story might even be prefaced with this point, e.g., 'The leaders in this company really care about the well-being of the employees.' The rest of the story then illustrates this.

Now, look at what Hubspot calls 'Our Story' on its website.

In 2004, we met as graduate students at MIT. While Brian was helping venture-backed start-ups with their go-to-market strategy, we started to notice something curious: Customers had gotten really good at blocking out interruptive marketing and sales tactics. The tried and true tactics of old (direct mail, email blasts, cold calls) simply weren't effective any more.

Meanwhile, Dharmesh's blog 'OnStartups' was seeing massive growth in traffic. We'll admit, we were surprised. How had this tiny blog with no budget generated more traffic than companies with professional marketing teams and way bigger budgets? It felt like a modern-day David versus Goliath.

So after many meetings, even more coffee, and the occasional Belgian beer (a shared favourite of ours) we came to the simple observation:

People don't want to be interrupted by marketers or harassed by salespeople. They want to be helped.

It was time to make the marketing and sales process human. Time to treat buyers like people, not numbers on a spreadsheet. Time to build an inbound community and help people achieve their business goals in a more personable, empathetic way.

We called it, HubSpot.

Now that is a story. It has time, place, causal sequence of events, characters (with their names) and a surprise ending.

So when you hear a story, or something that has the makings of a good story, you can use in business, look for the elements given above and you will surely have a complete story to tell.

4

Telling, Listening to and Triggering Stories

I N A REMOTE army installation in the Australian outback, amidst tents, bunkers, workshops, military vehicles, armoury and soldiers, are a bunch of civilians moving around with notebooks and clipboards. It's 2005 and Mark Schenk and Shawn Callahan from Anecdote are leading one of the two teams out to gather some data. The information is being collected in order to assess the training needs in the areas of operational health and safety for the Australian defence force.

One team is using a structured interview technique while the other is collecting stories about various aspects of behaviour.

After the first day on the field, the two teams meet to compare notes. The leader of the structured interview team says, 'At first blush, it seems like most things are in order. They are adhering to OH&S (occupational health and safety) processes. Sure, there are some areas for improvement, but generally things are okay.'

As the structured team continued describing its assessment, Shawn, who was leading the team collecting stories was surprised. He asked, 'So, you didn't hear about the soldiers who are showering in their own urine because their recycling system is broken, or about the workshop where everyone wears protective footwear because some poor fellow lost his toes in an accident but no one wears protective eyewear because they have never had an eye accident?'

While Shawn's team had collected numerous stories of major transgression, none of them were picked up in the structured interview approach.

The structured interviews have the advantage of efficiency since a large number of respondents are asked the same questions and hence responses can easily be collated and compared. However, the major disadvantage is that the interviewee may misrepresent the truth to make himself or herself seem more socially acceptable. This misrepresentation is avoided when you collect stories and check whether any pattern emerges from it before making your deduction. This is the power of 'story listening', a term coined by Shawn more than a decade ago.

'Tell me a story?' rarely gets people to narrate effortlessly as it immediately creates a pressure to perform. It is even more difficult if the question is asked in a business setting on an element of organizational behaviour. 'Tell me a story about unsafe practices in your division?' is likely to get a blank look at best. Story listening is the art of getting someone to tell a story effortlessly and organically. We will cover that technique and the many uses this skill can be put to in the chapters to come.

The work we do with stories in business has another element to it other than storytelling and story listening. It is what we call 'story triggering'. It involves leaders doing something remarkable which people in the organization will subsequently recount. 'Remarkable' is made up of two words—'remark' and 'able', i.e., worthy of a remark.

It was April 2001. I had just been appointed the regional sales manager for the northern region of the personal product division at Hindustan Unilever. I reached the Delhi office where the team took me through the yearly plan. We broke for lunch and proceeded to the canteen. As I was about to enter a hall that looked like a canteen, where many people were sitting at tables and eating, one of my managers warned in a loud whisper, 'No, no. Not that door', and pointed to a door adjacent to it. As I walked over to the other door and peered inside, I saw it looked similar. It was a hall with a lot of people sitting at tables and eating. I asked, 'What's the difference?' The reply I got was, 'That is the staff canteen and this is the one for managers.'

I was shocked as this was 2001 and not 1981. I was hoping my expression didn't make it too obvious. That evening, after my team left, I spent some time with the other regional sales managers, and we all agreed that there shouldn't be different canteens. The task of correcting that was easy as the only thing that separated the two canteens was a wall and a minor difference in cost per plate.

A few months later, I was on a market visit to Gorakhpur in eastern Uttar Pradesh. During a conversation with the distributor, he mentioned, 'We are very happy that that the current team of regional managers in Delhi believes in treating everyone equally.' I was surprised at the observation and asked, 'How do you know?' He smiled and said, 'You guys took down the wall between the staff and managers' canteen, didn't you?'

That story had travelled over 800 km to someone outside the company. The inference the distributor had made about us could never have been achieved had he, instead of hearing about the wall demolition, heard us assert that we believed in treating everyone equally.

We had inadvertently triggered a story.

While I did not know about the concept of story triggering in those days, it is a concept leaders would do well to be cognizant of. Instead of proclaiming their beliefs and asserting their character, it would be more powerful if leaders seized every opportunity to live the same and let other people come to their own conclusions.

Back in November 2014, I was having coffee with Viral Oza, the marketing director of Nokia, India, at the time. When we were talking about leadership styles of senior leaders we had worked with, the name Shiv Shivakumar came up. Shiv, who was appointed the chairman and CEO of PepsiCo, India, in 2013, was someone both of us had worked with. Viral had worked with him when he was the managing director at Nokia, and I had worked with him at Unilever.

Viral had heard from some friends in PepsiCo about a small change Shiv had made which had made a huge difference. Apparently, most PepsiCo CEOs before Shiv weren't very approachable. It was believed that as soon as the CEO would enter the office complex, a message would be relayed to the foyer. One of the lifts would be stopped and reserved for the CEO. As soon as the CEO would enter the building, he would be ushered into the lift and whisked away to the floor he sat on. There was an unwritten rule that no one else would take that lift. All that changed after Shiv joined. Instead of taking the lift, he would walk up to his floor every day, randomly stopping on several floors to say hello to the employees and ask about them and their work—a process that usually took no more than fifteen minutes. This behaviour convinced every PepsiCo employee that they had a new CEO who was approachable and cared about every individual. This was the belief even among employees who had never met Shiv. In fact, it was one such employee who had narrated this story to Viral. This story about Shiv's approach had not only travelled within PepsiCo but also outside of it. Someone at PepsiCo told Viral at Nokia, who told me, and I in turned narrated this to many others. Shiv had done something remarkable (remarkable—'worthy of being noticed especially as being uncommon or extraordinary', as per Merriam-Webster.com) and that had triggered stories about his character and his beliefs. There was no way Shiv could have achieved this by proclaiming he was a people's person, in town hall speeches or internal memos.

So, my invitation to you is to become the hero of stories that other people both inside and out of the organization talk about. It is from these stories that people will infer who you are and that inference will be imprinted in their minds.

As we progress, we will talk about all three aspects of stories. Let's start with storytelling.

I often get calls from managers leading the learning and development functions of organizations, asking me whether I will facilitate a programme on the 'art of storytelling'. My usual answer is no. I tell them I teach the science of storytelling.

Why do I do this? Isn't there an art to storytelling? Of course there is. But for all the storytelling required in business, we don't need to hone the skill all the way to make it an art. It would be great to start with basic steps—some processes and patterns that can help us consistently use the skill. Hence I call it the science of storytelling. It is a science when you repeat the activity and get the same result.

In helping you learn the science of storytelling, I am going to use the approach designed by Shawn and Mark. Just like many kids these days use those two training wheels attached to the rear wheel of a bicycle as they learn to balance, I have focused on four areas in business on which you can cut your storytelling teeth. For each of these four areas of business Shawn and Mark have developed a story pattern that can be used every time you need a story or a story structure for those situations.

This approach appeals to the people I have helped build the storytelling capability. Leaders with engineering and management degrees, and techies with a science background have somehow incorrectly convinced themselves that they are left-brained and anything to do with 'art' is beyond their ken. Their eyes light up when I tell them that we will work with science.

The four situations in business from where we start our storytelling journey are:

1. When we are building a rapport with people we hope to work with—clients, team members and stakeholders.
2. When we are explaining change—this could range from new vision, mission or transformation agenda to a small change in an administrative process.
3. When we are trying to get people to change their minds and when we are trying to handle objections or mental blocks.
4. When we are looking at sharing best practices, knowledge or success.

Once you are comfortable with these, you can take off the 'training wheels' and ride smoothly, and even do a few stunts. My belief is that in the long run, when you have started using the power of stories in many of your business conversations, these four structures will form 25 per cent or less of your story skills repertoire. More than 75 per cent of the time you will be using stories that you collect from the books you read, the people that you talk to and your own experience. You will use your story bank to explain complex information, share your vision or just drive home a point.

The next four chapters will help you learn the story skills that you can use in each of the above situations. We will then move on to looking at several business challenges that can be solved using different combinations of storytelling and story listening.

PART II

Different Story Patterns

5

Using Stories to Build Rapport and Credibility

Y<small>OU WILL AGREE</small> with me that people first need to buy you before they buy your product, service or idea. The question is: Do they buy your character or your credentials? The answer surely is character. As Shawn Callahan says, 'Character always trumps credentials.'

Imagine you are the local branch manager of a large multinational bank. I have just walked into your cabin looking for a working capital loan for my firm. I shake hands with you and say hello. I then sit down and launch into . . .

> Hi, my name is Indranil Chakraborty and I am the founder of StoryWorks. After completing my graduation in computer science and engineering at Jadavpur University in Kolkata, I did my postgraduation in management at the Indian Institute of Management Lucknow. I then joined . . .

Then I moved to retail . . . After that I worked . . . (I run through a mini version of my curriculum vitae [CV]).

After twenty-one years of corporate life, I started StoryWorks in 2013. I have been working very hard at evangelizing the concept of business storytelling across large corporates in this country. I am very passionate about the work I do and I have been meeting as many people as I can to grow this business. I'm confident that I have all that it takes to survive in an unstructured environment and grow a start-up. I'm certain that within the next few years StoryWorks will be one of the leading names in communication consulting in the country. In order to help us with our growing need for working capital, I am here to request for a working capital loan.

With that, I hand over the request form I had filled. How likely would you be to form an opinion about me based on everything I claimed to be—hard-working, networked, able to work in an unstructured environment, possessing an entrepreneurial drive and passionate? Chances are that you would be sceptical and may have even stifled a yawn or two. After all, we have been 'sold' to so many times that assertions are no longer credible. So you did get a litany of my credentials, but you got no real insight into my character.

Now imagine that you are the same bank manager, but instead of starting with my mini-CV-based introduction followed by assertions, I start like this:

Hi, my name is Indranil Chakraborty and I was born in Shillong, in the north-east of the country, to a middle-class family. Somehow, my parents managed to put me into a premier educational institute where almost all my classmates were from more affluent families than mine. And they always had more money to spend at the tuck shop—the canteen. So, when I was in class III, I started a comics' circulating library, that too with borrowed comics, and I did make a bit of money. Not as much as they had but much more than I ever had before. This excited me a lot and, ever since, doing something different to achieve a goal has always been very motivating. After finishing my schooling, I went to Jadavpur University in Kolkata to study computer science and engineering . . .

I then continue on my CV-based journey with another example or two about my passion for doing things on my own. The 16–17-second diversion about my comics' circulating library would have allowed you, the bank manager, to infer that I may have entrepreneurial skills, something that wouldn't have been possible had I claimed to possess that trait. And when you come to your own conclusion about this, you will value that much more than a close confidant telling you about my entrepreneurial skills.

By sharing small stories from my life, I can help my listeners understand what makes me tick and see if those character traits resonate with their own values and beliefs. That is when they start forming a bond. That is what we call a connection story.

Forming a bond is not only important when I am looking to convince you to give me a loan, but it is as important when as a speaker or presenter you are looking to grab the attention of your audience. After you gain the listeners' trust, they are more open to listening to your pitch.

Simon Sinek, the author of *Start with Why* and the speaker of one of the most viewed TED talks ever,[1] says, 'People don't buy what you do, people buy *why* you do it.' When we repeatedly share our *why*, we attract people who believe in what we believe, and when that happens trust emerges.

Will one story be enough to convince my listeners about a certain character trait? Surprisingly, it will. I have had over 2000 people try this at workshops and events, and it has always worked. This is because as far as our values and beliefs are concerned, people generally expect that if they see someone display a value once, that person would most likely display it all the time. Stephen Denning, the author of *The Leader's Guide to Storytelling*,[2] calls it 'the fractal nature of identifying stories'. Fractal is a mathematical term which describes a curve or geometrical figure, each part of which has the same statistical character as the whole.

I am often asked whether the connection story necessarily needs to be a defining moment in one's life. My answer is no, it need not be. Because of our consistency of behaviour around core values and beliefs, even a seemingly trivial incident can make the listener infer a lot about our character. You would have seen this in my 'comics' circulating library' example.

Here is another example from a story often told by Michael Dell, the founder of Dell, from when he was twelve years old:

The father of my best friend was a pretty avid stamp collector, so now naturally my friend and I wanted to collect stamps too. To fund my interest in stamps, I got a job as a water boy in a Chinese restaurant two blocks from my house. I started reading stamp journals just for fun, and soon began noticing that prices were rising. Before long, my interest in stamps began to shift from the joy of collecting to the idea that there was something here that my mother, a stockbroker, would have termed 'a commercial opportunity' . . .

I was about to embark upon one of my first business ventures. First, I got a bunch of people in the neighbourhood to consign their stamps to me. Then I advertised 'Dell's Stamps' in Linn's Stamp Journal, the trade journal of the day. And then I typed, with one finger, a twelve-page catalogue . . . and mailed it out. Much to my surprise, I made $2000. And I learnt an early, powerful lesson about the rewards of eliminating the middleman. I also learnt that if you've got a good idea, it pays to do something about it.[3]

We all know about Michael Dell's revolutionary direct-to-consumer success with personal computers and laptops. From the above incident, one can infer a lot about Dell's character. He was entrepreneurial, ambitious, aggressive and a risk taker—something we may not have believed had he just asserted that he had those traits.

Since different character traits are required to be amplified under different circumstances, we need different connection stories. The bank manager needed to know that I had entrepreneurial abilities, a client might need to know that I am flexible, a team member might need to know that I will always have his back. So, we need multiple connection stories in our collection.

How to Come Up with Connection Stories?

Shawn Callahan likes to ask people to think about three things in their lives that have shaped who they are today. These turning points could be from their professional or personal lives. A lot of our beliefs are formed, and our convictions tested, during significant life events, and so going back to such moments in time can definitely help us get stories about who we are.

I use a different approach with those who participate in my workshops, and I am going to walk you through those steps.

Take a piece of paper.

Did you get it? (You can even take a pencil and scribble on the template on the next page.) Now, start by thinking of a situation that may be coming up in the near future where you would be required to introduce yourself. Someone might be visiting you from the corporate office, you might be bringing onboard a new team member, or you may be meeting a new client or a new partner. Write down the situation on the top of the page. If you can't think of a real situation that will arise, imagine one.

Now write down five words or phrases about your character, values or beliefs that you would like your listener to infer about you in the first meeting. Some examples of such words or phrases could be—creative, innovative, diligent, entrepreneurial, someone who does not micromanage, someone who will always have his team members' backs, etc.

After you put down these five words or phrases, I want you to spend the next few minutes thinking about incidents in your life, from when you were a little child up until this day, and see if you can remember any incident where you displayed one or more of the five character traits you have put down.

If after running the show reel of your life in your mind's eye no incident pops up, try asking yourself the following questions: What were the events in your life where you saw tremendous success or failure? What were the moments in your life when you felt very proud? What are the things you love doing the most—outdoor activities, watching old movies, cooking, etc., and then think of why is it that you love doing these. You could also use Shawn's technique of thinking about some of the biggest turning points in your life.

I'm pretty certain that if you give yourself at least five minutes to mull over the situations and questions given above, you would have remembered more than one incident. Now write down a few words about one of the incidents on that piece of paper. It is your story and hence you don't have to write down everything. If I write down 'comics' circulating library' then I will remember the rest of the story, I don't have to write it all down.

Template for Finding a Connection Story

Situation: _____

Write down five words or phrases that you would like the listeners to infer about you. These could be values, beliefs or capabilities, e.g., honest, creative, hard-working, perseverant, dependable, etc.

_____

_____

_____

_____

_____

Think of a moment in time where you did something that demonstrates any *one* of the five traits listed above.

_____

_____

_____

_____

_____

After you've jotted down a few words that will remind you about the story, run it over in your head once more. Ask yourself what other character traits, values or beliefs would your listener infer about you when they hear your story. Stories are usually not unidimensional and hence even though you chose this story to demonstrate one trait, multiple character traits, values or beliefs are often displayed through a single incident. Jot the additional character traits that you feel people may take away from this story.

Now find someone who is willing to give you five minutes. Tell them that you will narrate an incident from your life, and you would like them to tell you what they infer about you from it. Remind them that they should only share what they infer from this story and not from their previous experience about you. Without telling them the context in which you will be using the story, just narrate it. 'When I was . . .'

After this, ask them to tell you what they inferred about you. Write it down on that piece of paper.

What did you observe? If you were like most of the participants in my workshops, your listener would have played back not only the character trait that made you choose the story but many other deductions too. That's how easy it is.

You may ask: How long should a connection story be? I prefer to chisel connection stories down to less than a minute and definitely no more than a minute and a half. Was your story more than two minutes long? Don't worry. Here are three steps you need to follow to make it concise.

First, tell the story to two other people. You will notice that your story will automatically become tighter. Why does this happen? Two reasons. One, as you hear yourself telling this story, you become conscious of elements that are not essential to the point you are making about yourself. Second, you are subconsciously picking up cues from your listeners. The listeners' body language, especially their eyes, gives your brain a continuous ECG-like reading about their interest. The next time you tell the story, the editing will automatically start.

The second thing you need to do is retell your story to yourself, but this time start with the character trait that you want your listener to take away. 'I have always been very creative. I remember when I was in school . . .' Voicing your intended takeaways will help you leave out everything that is superfluous to the core message.

The third thing I would like you to do is to record your story on your mobile phone and transcribe it. Then, go line by line, word by word and keep asking yourself if all the words are necessary to get the point across. Many a time, like amateur writers, we fall in love with a certain section of our story and continue to carry it along even if it is not required. Imagine that I had named my comics' circulating library 'The Phantom in the Classroom' and was very proud of my creativity. If I am not conscious, this is something I would definitely want to mention when I narrate my story. But is it essential to making the point that I have entrepreneurial inclinations? Not at all, which is why it needs to be dropped.

Following these three steps usually gets a story down to a bare minimum without losing the character trait you want to convey.

Sometimes, when we share our connection stories during our 'test drives', we may get a feedback about a trait that surprises us. While the mention of a positive nature would be great, being told about a negative trait makes it easy to spot the elements that leave that impression. Then you evaluate whether it is possible, not to compromise on the authenticity but to remove or reduce the focus on that element without losing the essence of the story.

One of the connection stories I use is about the time when I was doing very well at Hindustan Unilever. I had got many accolades and awards, and I thought that I was well on my way to becoming a 'CEO by forty'. That is when I was diagnosed with bipolar disorder or hypomania. The next year was spent in treatment and recuperation. After I came out of it, I was fairly bitter. Almost all my conversations went into 'life is unfair, what did I do to deserve this, etc'. It took a story that a mentor told me to come out of that zone and throw away the baggage. Once that was done, I was able to focus on my job and get my career back on track. When I narrate this story and ask people what they inferred about me, they tell me positive things about resilience, learning from experience, being open to feedback, etc. When I first shared this story with a friend, he too spoke about similar things but added that I whined a lot. I was taken aback! I am not a whiner. So I replayed the story and realized that during my narration, I had spoken about my belief at that time that 'life was unfair' four times. I had said 'when I met my friends I always maintained life was unfair, this shouldn't have happened to me', 'when I met my colleagues I told them that I did not deserve this', 'once when I went for a reunion and my old classmates asked me how I was doing, I defensively went into 'life is unfair, etc'. When I realized this, I ensured that I didn't say this so many times. After that, I have used this connection story over fifty times on formal occasions and never got negative feedback about whining.

Sometimes, the challenge is to tell a story that doesn't sound like you are blowing your own trumpet. One approach is to take the spotlight off yourself and play the supporting role, making someone else play the lead role.

One such story I have often used is how, back in 2011, I was struggling to find a way to embed, across the breadth of the company, some newly created organizational values. I thought running value workshops across the organization would be the solution, but much to my horror, I found out six months later that less than 5 per cent of the employees really understood and lived those values. The values we had created, like in many other companies, had become just a plaque on the wall. My search for a better solution led me to Mark Schenk and Shawn Callahan, who subsequently introduced me to the art of storytelling and story listening as a great way to embed values. The success of this process was so phenomenal that I decided to quit my job and start my own organization to bring the power of stories to businesses in Asia.

So, Mark and Shawn are the front and centre of this story. They are the stars, but I play a significant supporting role. When I ask my listeners what they infer about me after hearing this story, they usually say:

1. You are passionate about storytelling.
2. You are willing to take risks.
3. You are perseverant.
4. You have experience of working in large organizations.
5. You are confident enough to share your mistakes.
6. You are experienced in storytelling.

I never get the sense that they think I'm boasting. On the contrary, it feels like we make a connection quickly, and our relationship is off to a good start.

So, think about those times when you have lent a helping hand, where you have helped create conditions for others to succeed, where you have displayed many other traits that are central to who you are and tell these stories to introduce yourself and build a rapport.

One of the things we must guard against is the desire to use an incident that is not true but borrowed from some trait we admired in someone else. An inauthentic story will soon be exposed when your subsequent behaviour doesn't demonstrate the same, and then you will be branded as a charlatan and an untruthful storyteller.

This is also where we must be cognizant of 'invented memory'—memory of events that never happened or did not happen in that manner, but because we have told it so many times we start believing it to be true. As Jonathan Gottschall said in his book, *The Storytelling Animal*:[4]

> A life story is not, however, an objective account. A life story is a carefully shaped narrative that is replete with strategic forgetting and skilfully spun meanings.

He goes on to say that life stories should come with a disclaimer: 'This story that I tell about myself is only based on a true story. I am in large parts a figment of my own yearning imagination.'

It is a good idea to check the story, wherever possible, with other people who were part of it in order to ensure that the story does not have any elements of 'yearning imagination'.

The final caution to be exercised when it comes to a connection story is that we must always repeat the 'test drive' of our connection story when we change the audience, especially when we are addressing an audience from a different culture.

One of the stories I use to let listeners infer that I am bold and not afraid to speak my mind is an incident that occurred in 1998.

> Six years into my first job, when I was still a junior manager, I got into an argument with the head of business during

dinner after the launch of a strategy. I was arguing that I didn't believe one leg of the strategy would work, and I was forcefully trying to make the point. The next morning, a helpful colleague asked me why I was hell-bent on having what he called a 'career limiting conversation'. But I think that conversation had a positive effect. Two weeks after that, I was chosen, by the same head of business, to lead a cross-functional team to work out plans to execute parts of the strategy. I don't think that would have happened had the business head been offended.

While this incident, when narrated in India, gets me the desired feedback about being bold and my lack of fear to speak my mind, it is not a story I would use in Thailand where it is considered rude to disagree with someone in public.

The power of connection stories can be summarized with one thought. When a stand-up comedian goes up on stage, he or she does not start by saying, 'Hi everybody, I am a really funny guy here to entertain you.' No, he or she tells us a joke.

While so far I have focused on using connection stories to build a rapport when meeting new people, personal stories are also a very powerful way in which leaders can demonstrate that they are very much like the people they lead. Just like their colleagues, the leaders too can show that they are just as human and hold similar values and beliefs.

Why is this important? While we have for decades heard that 'opposites attract', new studies across the world have come to the conclusion that we are attracted to people who are similar to us. We tend to gravitate towards and trust people like ourselves.

Simon Sinek made a forceful point about this in his speech at the Adobe Conference, 99U, in 2012.[5] He asserted before his largely American audience that if any of them were visiting Paris and heard someone around them speaking with an American accent, they would surely ask, 'Hey, where are you guys from?' And if they were told, 'We're from Los Angeles', the response might be 'Oh my God! We're from New York.' And then both the groups would bond immediately. If someone in the other group recommended a fantastic Italian restaurant that should not be missed, it would surely be added to the to-do list. Simon then said, 'I find this very funny because if a Frenchman turned to you and randomly said, welcome to our country; you should try this restaurant, you'd be like, "You're a weirdo. What're you telling us this for? We are not going there." Even though there is a higher chance that he would know something off the beaten path.'

We are more likely to believe and trust people like us than someone who we think is not like us.

Think back to the time when you joined your first job as an intern. In your first few months, what did your CEO appear to be like? Like you or very different?

Imagine that today is your first day at your first job. You are a management trainee at PepsiCo. What does Indra Nooyi, the Global CEO, appear to be? Someone far removed from who you are, someone closer to God than human, someone on a pedestal? How do such leaders try and get close to you and show you that they are like you?

Now imagine you are attending an induction programme for trainees across the world, Indra Nooyi is at the podium, and she shares this story:

This is about fourteen years ago. I was working in the office. I work very late, and we were in the middle of the Quaker Oats acquisition. I got a call about 9.30 p.m. from the existing chairman and CEO at that time. He said, 'Indra, we're going to announce you as president and put you on the board of directors.' I was overwhelmed. Look at my background and where I come from—to be president of an iconic American company and to be on the board of directors—I thought something special had happened to me.

'So rather than stay and work until midnight, which I normally would've done because I had so much work to do, I decided to go home and share the good news with my family. I got home about 10 p.m. I got into the garage, and my mother was waiting at the top of the stairs. And I said, 'Mom, I've got great news for you.'

'Let the news wait. Can you go out and get some milk?'

I looked into the garage and it looked like my husband was home. I said, 'What time did he get home?'

'8 p.m.'

'Why didn't you ask him to buy the milk?'

'He's tired'

'Okay. We have a couple of helps at home. Why didn't you ask them to get the milk?'

'I forgot. Just get the milk. We need it for the morning.'

So like a dutiful daughter, I went out and got the milk. I banged it on the counter and said, 'I had great news for you. I've just been told that I'm going to be president and on the board of directors. And all that you want me to do is go out and get milk. What kind of a mom are you?' And she said to me, 'Let me explain something to you. You might be the president of PepsiCo, you might be on the board of directors, but when you enter this house, you're a wife, you're a daughter, you're a daughter-in-law, you're a mother, you're all of that. Nobody else can take that place. So leave that damned crown in the garage. And don't bring it into the house.'[6]

Now, as that PepsiCo intern, don't you think that Indra Nooyi had walked down from the pedestal to someone closer to you, someone who is almost like you.

So whether it is building a rapport with someone you are meeting for the first time or when you are trying to get closer to the people you lead, sharing anecdotes from your life can be a very powerful tool.

6

Using Stories to Influence and Overcome Objections

IN A SEMINAL study conducted at Stanford University, researchers put together two groups of students who had diametrically opposite views on capital punishment. Half of them believed that the death penalty was a deterrent, while the other half believed that it had no effect on crime.

These students were then provided data from two opposing studies. One provided argument and evidence that supported the deterrence belief while the other provided argument and evidence that questioned the same. Both the studies had actually been made up by the researchers and were designed to provide equally compelling data. Results showed that both the proponents and opponents became more polarized in their opinions. The students who had originally supported the death penalty felt that that the pro-deterrence data was very convincing, and that the anti-deterrence data was not convincing at all. The other students felt exactly the opposite. In fact, when asked to compare their current attitude towards the death penalty with the attitude they had at the beginning of the experiment, the proponents reported that they were even more convinced that the death penalty was a deterrent, whereas the opponents reported being doubly convinced against it.

This experiment goes to show that we suffer from cognitive bias—a mistake in reasoning that often occurs as a result of holding on to one's beliefs regardless of contrary information. This is a phenomenon called 'belief perseverance'.

I remember reading a story about elephants and chains many years ago. It goes like this:

> A man was passing by an elephant enclosure in a zoo when he noticed that the huge animals were being restricted using only a small rope tied to their front leg. There were no chains and no cages. Clearly, these elephants could break out of these bonds without much effort. The man was intrigued and asked the mahout about it. The mahout smiled and said, 'Right from the time when the elephants are small, we use the same rope to tie them. At that age, this rope is enough to hold them. As they grow up, they are conditioned to believe they cannot break away. They believe that the same rope can still restrain them, so they never try to break free.'

Isn't that amazing? The elephants are not the only ones bound by the story in their heads. It happens to all of us, and it also happens in organizations. Belief perseverance can help us understand why it is so hard to change entrenched views. All of us who have tried to implement any change—change in culture, transformation, new approach or strategy—would certainly have faced this challenge. This is why when individuals, teams and employees in an organization believe in something contrary to the change one is trying to incorporate, the resistance is enormous.

The usual approach to change starts with our own belief that people are rational, and that when we reach out to them using reason, facts and logic they will come around, but surprisingly, they often do not. We also assume that a powerful, impassioned speech accompanied by a jazzy PowerPoint presentation will do the trick. When it doesn't, we try even harder. We think we just need to find the correct argument, and putting more hard facts on the table will work. But it doesn't.

Clearly, pushing data and analysis isn't enough when the listener has a story in his head. This is something we call an anti-story, a story the listener has in his head as to why what is being proposed will not work. One can't use data and logic when debating against someone who has an anti-story because one can never replace a story with facts, no matter how robust and statistically significant they might be. We can only replace it with a more powerful story. As philosopher Gordon Livingston said more articulately, 'It is difficult to remove by logic an idea not placed there by logic in the first place.'

Now, let us look at a different approach.

In 2010, after the global financial crisis, the US Federal Reserve chief Ben Bernanke appeared on the show *60 Minutes* on CBS News to persuade Americans to bail out the banking system. Instead of pushing a bunch of data and analysis, he used a metaphor. 'Imagine', he explained, 'that you had an irresponsible neighbour who smoked in bed and set fire to his house. Should you call the fire department, or should you simply walk away and let him face the consequences of his actions? What if your house—indeed all the houses in the entire neighbourhood—were also made of wood? We all agree that under those circumstances, we should focus on putting out the fire first. Then we can turn to the issues of assigning blame or punishment, rewriting the fire code and putting fail-safe in place'.

This is a very powerful analogy. It communicated the clear and present danger to the economy and the urgency of implementing his proposed solution. Denise Cummins, the author of *Good Thinking: Seven Powerful Ideas That Influence the Way We Think*,[1] believes that analogies and metaphors are a powerful way to change our minds. We can't help noticing that 'this is like that' and arguments that exploit this natural tendency tend to hold sway.

Narrating a real event is even more powerful than analogies and metaphors. While analogies and metaphors are hypothetical and plausible, stories are real. This adds to the impact they have.

So then, the trick lies in not *pushing* data and analysis as the only way to change people's mind but painting a picture of the alternative universe we believe in and letting the listener *pull* it in. And then, when he is more open to receiving the information, we share data and analyses that support our view. Stories are a 'pull strategy' because the listener uses the details in the story to create a picture in his or her own mind. The listener 'owns' the story and it does not trigger the confirmation bias.

Anantha Radhakrishnan, CEO of Infosys BPM, says that this is the best way to introduce an opposing point. 'Whenever I jump straight into questioning someone else's view or sharing a different view, people get extremely defensive and almost stop listening,' he says. 'But when I start with a story, there is nothing to argue against. People are open to listening, and then I link the takeaway from the story to the point I am making.'

Try this approach and see how effective the result is.

In the work I do, we have discovered that the story approach is very powerful. I use a communication pattern called the 'Influence' story pattern.

I start by acknowledging the story the listener has in his or her head, the anti-story. I then share an anecdote where the point of view I have has actually worked before putting forth my case and making my point.

Here is an example. There are times when people tell me, 'The work you are doing in business storytelling seems very intuitive and very powerful. But I am not sure it will work in my industry (construction, aerospace, insurance, etc.).'

When I am faced with this, the influence story I use goes like this:

1. **Acknowledge the Anti-Story:** 'Given how new the field of business storytelling is, I can see how you might be sceptical about its usage in your industry.'
2. **Share the Story of the Opposite Point of View:** 'About a year ago, I was speaking to the chief human resource

officer of a major power company. He had exactly the same doubts. In fact, he went on to add, "We are neither a typical business-to-business, nor a business-to-consumer company. We generate electricity and supply to captive consumers." I insisted that great communication is not just required for external stakeholders but perhaps even more important for the internal ones. A great team works on engines oiled by great communication. He agreed to run a pilot programme and test the ground with twenty of his senior managers. The programme was so successful that we have now rolled it out to everyone at the senior level and are working on taking it to the next level.'

3. **Make the Case:** 'Hence, I strongly feel that the power of stories cuts across functions and industries. Wherever communication is important, stories can be an extremely effective, game-changing tool.'

4. **Make the Point:** 'So I would urge you to try out this new skill and see for yourself how we are all hardwired for stories.'

I must confess that this influence story may not have converted every sceptic, but more than half of them have changed their minds.

The anecdotes we use need not be a success story. Any incident that can trigger a thought that questions the listener's status quo will work.

Let me give you an example.

Vineet (name changed) is the learning and development head assisting the business development team of a large professional service firm that is focused on delivering digital transformation for its client. They do this by helping clients set up and run advance processes and operations based on technology. This year, Vineet's plate is full and his training calendar is choc-a-bloc. He needs to enhance the team's capability around design thinking, machine learning and artificial intelligence. I met him to explain how harnessing the power of stories could help his business development team get even better at engaging, influencing and inspiring their clients. He was very keen to listen. He saw the power of using all the story types—connection, clarity, influence and success—and understood how it could really benefit the business leadership team. However, he had a constraint. He said, 'There are already too many items on my training calendar, and I am not sure that prioritizing storytelling over some of the other interventions would be worth it. After all, those have been identified as key after a lot of deliberation.'

I then shared with Vineet a similar conversation I had a year ago. Last year, I was talking to Ravi (name changed) who was the head of business development in Company X (a company in the same industry). I told Vineet that Ravi had invested a lot of effort and time the previous year in getting his team up to speed with the latest in various technologies and digital advancements. These were all areas that were crucial to differentiating between their offerings to their clients. But it didn't seem to have any of the desired effects. While they were able to demonstrate their understanding of the subject in quizzes and role plays, they didn't seem to be able to share that in client conversations. So, he had decided to repeat the training to reinforce the knowledge and understanding. I asked him, 'What do you think the problem is? Is it really lack of knowledge and understanding or a lack of confidence and ability to explain?' This got Ravi thinking and he said, 'You are right. They seem to be able to explain these advanced concepts to people like themselves but struggle when they need to do the same for people not from an IT background, for people from the business side.'

'So, what I hear you saying is that they do understand the concepts they were taught but were unable to communicate the same to a novice.'

'Exactly.'

'Then, what your business development team needs is not reinforcing the technical knowledge but help in building the ability to communicate the same to non-technical people.'

'You may be right.'

'Then you need to invest in helping them build their communication skills.'

What I had shared with Vineet was not a success story. It would have been a success story had I managed to get Ravi to run programmes on storytelling for the business development team. However, replaying my conversation with Ravi got Vineet wondering about whether he needed to think differently.

Our mind is full of beliefs, assumptions and opinions. In Vineet's case, it was about a belief that technical know-how was the only important skill required. Most such beliefs are created by experiences we have had or stories we have heard. Vineet must have experienced success in the past by focusing primarily on technical knowledge. Repeating these stories and what it means for us usually cements the same and creates our world view.

The best way someone else can plant a seed of doubt is by painting the picture of an alternative reality and letting us question ours. Slowly, this questioning and openness to an existence of a different possibility is the only way we can change our minds. That alternative reality is provided by the influence story that is shared.

Use the space below to try out an influence story of your own.

Think of an entrenched view in your team or organization that is causing friction or reducing effectiveness. Now use the influence story structure to create a communication to address it.

Acknowledge the anti-story _____

_____

_____

_____

_____

Share an example of a story of the opposite being true _____

_____

_____

_____

_____

Make your case. Summarize the key takeaway of the above story, the opposite point of view _____

_____

_____

_____

_____

_____

Make your point. This is your ask, i.e., 'This is why I feel you should . . .' _____

_____

_____

_____

_____

_____

7

Getting Strategies to Stick

ABOUT 120 OF your top managers have gathered in the ballroom of a hotel in an exotic location. It's your annual conference and you have a strategic road map to share. Your organization's head of strategy has worked long hours with you to ensure that the message that goes out is just right. Finally, your chief marketing officer and your advertising agency have put together a presentation that is visually rich. Now, it's your turn, as a chief executive, to deliver the speech and get 120 people to align with your strategy and make it work.

You practised your speech many times and that, along with the powerful presentation, was a big hit. Many in the audience said so after the speech and during the evening celebrations. This was perhaps the maximum number of acknowledgements you received for any of the annual strategy road map presentations you have made over the years.

Two weeks later, the euphoria of a fabulous conference is over, and you're at a regional meeting where fifteen of the managers who attended the conference are present. You do a random check to see how many of them remembered the strategic road map and understood how it applied to them. How many of them got it right? Well, if two or more got it, you have beaten the odds. In the book *The Strategy-Focused Organization*, Robert Kaplan and David Norton[1] note that, according to research data, on an average only 5 per cent of the workforce understand their company's strategy.

The situation becomes even worse when the message needs to be taken down to the next level. A version of the CEO's PowerPoint presentation is sent out to the regional offices along with detailed speaker notes. Has that ever worked in the organizations you have worked with? In my earlier years at work, I have been a recipient of many such decks. My manager would connect his laptop to the projector and say, 'I have been asked by the head office to share this strategy presentation which was shared with us in Goa last week.' He would then go on reading slide after slide with a few sheepish pauses and comments of 'I am not sure what this means.' We would all be suitably bored and happy when the presentation got over. If 5 per cent was the retention after the real event, you can well imagine what the comprehension and retention of the strategy would have been after a second-hand presentation.

I have seen two very different but amusing reactions when I ask employees in client organizations, 'Can you tell me a couple of the key themes of your annual strategy?' The senior people dive into their laptops saying, 'Give me a moment, I have a copy of the PPT.' The juniors just shrug and smile.

Why do such important messages not stick? There are three key reasons:

1. Abstraction of language.
2. Absence of context.
3. The curse of knowledge.

Abstraction of Language

In Chapter 2, I discussed at length the love many of us have for business jargon. Jargon seems to have a viral life of its own. A smooth-talking leader or manager comes up with a unique way of expressing something—'growth hacking' or 'this is the Uber for X' or 'Y is the new oil' and then hundreds of others cling on to it for dear life. It is unnecessary cleverness followed by exponential echoing.

In April 2018, Elon Musk, co-founder and CEO of Tesla, sent an email to Tesla employees. In it he mentions seven productivity recommendations. One of them reads 'Don't use acronyms or nonsense words for objects, software or processes at Tesla. In general, anything that requires an explanation inhibits communication. We don't want people to have to memorize a glossary just to function at Tesla.'

I know I have been as guilty of abstraction as anyone else. Somehow when my designation included the term 'chief strategy officer', I lost the ability to speak simple English when sharing strategy. Surely, I wasn't being paid so much money to be simple. Could I just say that 'this year one of the key areas we will drive is teamwork?' No. It would sound much more strategic if I said, 'This year, we need to break the silos across the business and foster a sense of deep trust and collaboration across all verticals of the company.'

It is precisely abstractions like these that are the reason why messages don't stick.

Any of us who have heard Steve Jobs's speeches at the World Wide Developer Conferences (WWDCs) know that we remember a lot of it even weeks after viewing it.

In linguistics, the Gunning Fog Index (GFI) is a readability test for English writing. The index estimates the years of formal education a person needs to understand the text on the first reading. A GFI of 12 requires the reading level of a U.S. high school senior (around eighteen years old). Some analysts took the transcripts of keynote speeches given by Steve Jobs, Michael Dell and Bill Gates in 2007. The GFI for Jobs's transcript was rated at 5.5, Dell at 9.1 and Gates at a whopping 10.7. This means that while one requires 5.5 years of formal education to understand Steve Jobs's speech, one would need 10.7 years of formal education to understand the one delivered by Bill Gates. No wonder one understands and remembers Steve Jobs's keynotes so easily.

Absence of Context

An unverified story about poet and novelist Victor Hugo tells us that just after the publication of *Les Misérables*, impatient to learn of the success of the book, he sent off a letter which contained only the following:

?

He received an entirely satisfactory answer from his publisher, Hurst & Blackett:

!

This cryptic communication worked well only because the context was extremely clear to both parties.

Context is critical because it tells you, the receiver, what importance to place on something, what assumptions to draw (or not) about what is being communicated, and most importantly, it puts meaning into the message.

This brings us to the second barrier to stickiness of our message—the illusion of transparency. We often think that others are much more in sync with what we are thinking than they really are. And hence we jump straight into the 'what' of our message without even a tiny mention of the 'why'. This is accentuated when we are speaking to people in our own company. Psychologists call it the signal amplification bias. We routinely fail to realize how little we are actually communicating.

Many a times when I have brought this to the attention of the speaker, I have heard, 'I thought it was obvious that . . .' or, 'I didn't think I needed to spell that out.' I know it is easier for me, an outsider to spot this, but being aware of this as a communicator would certainly help.

Understanding the context becomes even more critical when the message is about change. We are biased towards reason. We feel that even if we don't like to do what we are being told to do, it becomes easier to complete the task once we are given the reason behind why we are doing it.

This was brilliantly demonstrated in an experiment conducted at the Harvard University, which showed that people were twice as likely to allow others to jump a queue when given a reason compared to when not given any. That is the power of 'why'.[2]

A lot of our internal communication assumes context and that is the second reason why such messages lack memorability.

Curse of Knowledge

The third is a phenomenon called the 'curse of knowledge', as illustrated brilliantly in an experiment by Stanford University graduate student, Elizabeth Newton, in 1990.[3] Elizabeth took 240 students and divided them into two groups. One group played the role of tappers and the other group were listeners. Each tapper was given a well-known English song such as 'Jingle Bells', and their job was to tap out the rhythm on a table. The listener's job was to guess the song. The experiment began after each tapper was paired with a listener.

At the end, the tappers were asked to predict the probability of their partners having guessed the song. The average prediction was 50 per cent. The reality was that the listeners guessed correctly only 2.5 per cent of the times. Why did this happen? The curse of knowledge! When the tune was playing in the tapper's head, the tapping seemed to be a perfect match, but for the listener, who did not have the tune in his or her head, it sounded like random noise. The tappers were usually shocked about how difficult it was for the listeners to get it right.

The challenge is that once we know something—like the tune of a song—we find it hard to imagine the others not knowing it. Our knowledge curses us into a delusion about clarity.

Just like the tappers and listeners, in the business world, the provider of the strategy message (you) and the receivers (your employees) are perhaps in a situation of information asymmetry. During the time when I was working in corporates and was senior enough to be responsible for transformation and strategy, I fell for the same trap. I would work with my team for weeks on the strategy. By the time of the event where I would need to share it, the strategy (the tune) would be running in my head. During the conference, I would jump on to the stage and do the corporate version of tapping—bullet points on a PowerPoint presentation. I would then come off the stage thinking that since it was an easy song (the strategy), and I was a brilliant tapper (tapping out the bullet points), the audience would have got it. But I don't think I ever broke the 5 per cent barrier.

The solution: this is where narratives can come to the rescue. In our practice, we call it 'clarity stories'. It usually has four parts:

1. In the past.
2. Then something happened.
3. So now.
4. In the future.

The narrative begins with setting the context. What is it that you were doing in the past and what results did you see. Most of this is usually positive. After all, we have been a successful company. But then something changed. The change could be internal or external. This part of the narrative includes both the factors that are forcing us to change and the elements that are enabling us to change. We then talk about the change itself and the new behaviours it requires us to have. Finally, the narrative ends with painting a picture of what would happen in the future, of what success would look like to people within the company and all the stakeholders without. Let me illustrate the four parts with an example: an IT head explaining the stringent requirement to change the password every seven days.

> *In the past*, we were just a small biopharmaceutical company. Most people hadn't heard of us. This was also a time when we issued all the devices our employees used— laptops and mobile phones. Since these were standard issues, we were able to install the relevant firewalls and data-protection software. Additionally, all our data was housed in servers that were on our premises, and the only way to connect to them was through the office LAN. Everything was secure.
>
> *Then, something happened*. Over the last seven years, we have grown to become the third-largest company in this space. In fact, we have been filing more patents every year than any of our competitors. Today, our products are sold in more than a 100 countries. This position makes us an attractive target for hackers. There

are a lot of people out there who would pay good money for the information we have. We have already seen two hacker attacks this year, and while we have been able to ensure that there was only minimal damage, we had to deal with significant downtime and needed to divert resources to fight these attacks. Over the years, a lot of things have changed internally as well. We now have a BYOD—bring your own device—policy. Hence, we have several laptop models and operating systems being used by employees. In fact, the youngsters seem to be changing their mobile phones every six months. It is virtually impossible to install reliable data protection solutions for each and every one of them. And to add to the complexity of protection, all our data is now stored in the cloud and employees are accessing it from everywhere—at office, at home, at Starbucks. This has increased our vulnerability.

So now, we are mandating that all the devices have to be password-protected, all system access has to be password-protected. The password would need to be changed every seven days, failing which, the device would be locked and access to our systems will be denied.

In the future, this move will ensure that we will be far less vulnerable to intrusions and can focus our energies on our core business. I am also happy to make a commitment here. If we see very high levels of compliance to this mandate, I am open to moving to a single password for all our various systems. This way, you will need to remember and change only two passwords—your device and the universal systems access.

Benefits of Using a Clarity Story

We all get stories. No matter what our experience in the organization is, no matter what our education levels are, and how deep our industry understanding is, we all get stories. The fact that we don't use complex words and abstract jargons when telling stories only helps.

When we share the strategy as a narrative, we are able to harness three powers of stories: they are easy to understand, easy to remember and easy to retell. There are several advantages to this process.

Everyone uses the same narrative structure or skeleton when talking about the strategy. So, sharing the strategy is no longer subjected to the interpretation of various senior members of the team. Whether the CEO is addressing the annual conference today or the CFO is having a regional finance heads meet tomorrow, or the CMO is addressing all the marketing and agency personnel the day after, they are all using the same narrative structure and, hence, there is consistency.

Consistency is a critical element in getting messages to stick. Though everyone is using the same narrative structure, we teach them to find personal experiences and anecdotes to illustrate parts of the narrative. Moments that exemplify the point they are making. This brings richness to the tapestry of the story.

The third advantage is the most powerful—stories can be retold. No matter how clear your message is, and how simple it is to understand, there are only a limited number of occasions, be it one-to-one or one-to-many, for you (or your team) to personally narrate the strategic story to your employees.

However, a story well told is easy to retell, and this strategic story can be retold by the people whom you tell the story to. In turn, they can tell it to others. Finally, we have a cascade that works. And your strategy sticks.

Addressing Anti-Stories

What are anti-stories? Anti-stories are stories that listeners in the audience have in their heads about why a proposed strategy, process, change or transformation will not work. This is not just among the cynics and not always malicious. Often, such observations are based on historic evidence.

What Kryptonite is to Superman, anti-stories are to any communication exercise. Especially those dealing with change.

How often, during the coffee breaks between a conference, have you heard groups discussing why something a leader has proposed cannot be done? Cannot be done in this company, in this industry, in this country, etc.

Annette Simmons, a leading expert in business storytelling, got it absolutely right when she titled her book *Whoever Tells the Best Story Wins.*[4] Stories based on something that actually happened in the past are usually more powerful than the stories we want to write about how the future will be.

Conversations on unacknowledged and unaddressed anti-stories don't vanish after the communication event. They just move to the water cooler.

That is why, after the clarity story is developed, we need to identify possible anti-stories for the changes that we propose. Very often, a tuned-in senior management will know what the anti-stories are. However, for very large transformation projects and when the people putting together the strategy do not know the audience very well—new management, merged or acquired company, etc.—it is advisable to probe around to check whether there are anti-stories linked to the change themes. One way to find out is to do some exercises in story listening. This technique is described in Chapter 9.

In 2014, while working on a clarity story of transformation for one of the largest media organizations in the world, I conducted story-listening exercises to find out if there were any anti-stories.

One of the legs of the transformation strategy was 'to build state-of-the-art IT infrastructure so that manual repetitive work can be replaced with technology'. The time freed up would allow employees to do value-added work. During my story-listening sessions, I heard several stories whose pattern was 'our IT systems are so bad that it takes us five days to get client-wise profitability, and that too most of the times the first iteration is wrong. You remember what happened with the data we asked for three weeks ago?'

Now imagine what would happen if during their annual conference the CEO unveiled the transformation strategy and shared the thrust on 'IT to replace repetitive work', but did not address the anti-story about the current state of affairs. For sure, during the first coffee break, many people would have said, 'IT to replace my repetitive work? They can't even give us client-wise profitability . . .' These conversations plant a seed of doubt in the listeners' minds. If this story is well told, it will win over the new story about the future the CEO has been trying to tell. Remember, whoever tells the best story wins.

So, how do you handle anti-stories? Using hierarchical power, refuting the anti-story and saying it's not true doesn't work. Neither does circulating facts like the last quarter's actual turnaround time on profitability calculations. We believe that we can never fight an anti-story with a fact, we can only replace it with a better story.

This is best done using the influence story structure I described in Chapter 6. The first step is to acknowledge the presence of the anti-story and then put a more powerful story in its place. In the case of the transformation strategy story being narrated by the CEO, he spoke about the 'IT to replace repetitive work' leg of the strategy and paused. He looked at the audience and said, 'Now some of you must be thinking, "How on earth are we going to do something so big when it sometimes takes us five days to get client-wise profitability?" We recognized the problem and decided to do something about it. As we speak, teams from Company A (a renowned software consulting businesses) and Company B (one of the world's best IT implementers) are auditing our entire system. The CEOs of both these companies have personally committed to me that they will put in place a world-class system across the organization in nine months.'

With that, the anti-story was replaced. Now, the water cooler conversation would not have an impact as people would have another story.

One of the best confirmations of having identified a powerful anti-story is when you hear nervous laughter from the audience as you acknowledge the anti-story. It is almost like you caught them thinking about something bad.

My favourite way of addressing an anti-story is the 'mea culpa strategy'.

The best example I have seen is the first five minutes of Steve Jobs's speech at the WWDC of 2011, where he introduced iCloud. There was clearly a huge anti-story about MobileMe, a previous attempt by Apple on online services, which had failed to live up to Apple's reputation of reliability and user-friendliness, with more glitches than features.

He anticipated the possible anti-story and tackled it beautifully by saying, 'Now you might ask "Why would we believe them? They are the ones that brought me MobileMe."' The audience erupted in laughter. He then said, 'It wasn't our finest hour, but we've learnt a lot.' He went on to narrate the story of how the new iCloud architecture was built. With that simple approach, he took the heat out of this huge anti-story.

The mea culpa strategy, firstly, is knowing that the story is a problem—it's a barrier to your strategy—and then admitting it.

Ignoring or denying an anti-story only increases its power, it's like pouring petrol on a fire. The anti-story becomes even more difficult to dislodge.

Once the narrative is ready, the best way to communicate is orally.

So, use the clarity story whenever you are explaining any change—be it something as big as an annual strategy or as small as a change in the product you are selling. See how people easily understand it, remember it and are able to retell it days and weeks after you have shared it with them.

Use the space below to try out a clarity story of your own.

Think of a change initiative you are trying to drive in your team or in society. Now use the clarity story structure to create a communication to inform and align your listeners.

In the past _____

_____

_____

_____

_____

Then something happened _____

_____

_____

_____

_____

So now (this is where you talk about not just the 'what' but also the 'how' and the 'by when') _____

_____

_____

_____

_____

In the future _____

_____

_____

_____

_____

8

Writing Case Studies That Are Understood, Remembered and Can Be Retold

R EAD, PREFERABLY ALOUD, the following paragraphs either till the end or till you get bored. Then skip to the end.

The client is a media company involved in developing high-profile, lifestyle-oriented content for many media platforms, including television, digital, mobile and publishing. They wanted to optimize and monetize multiple streams of content, but were facing workflow performance issues such as low throughput, slow content processing and processing errors during heavy load.

Our team of experts was facilitating digital content management for the media company. We were responsible for indexing, converting, transforming and delivering media assets for consumption across different customer platforms. However, asset processing speeds were very low. A two-GB video was taking twenty minutes for processing, thus allowing the media house to publish only seventy-two assets in a day. This was resulting in limited business.

Our team came up with an out-of-the-box solution. They suggested replacing the current single-threaded asset model for video transcoding with a multi-threaded one. Multi-threaded execution enabled parallel processing of new and cached assets, thereby increasing the number of videos getting processed in a day and generating more business for the customer.

After our team made this architectural change, the media house started processing over 750 two-GB videos every day, hence increasing its total business ten fold. This small idea has been generating close to $6 million of additional revenue a year. This achievement was recognized by the client as one of the top ten revenue-generating ideas of the year.

This is an executive summary of a four-page case study that was being used by a leading IT company in India to showcase innovative thinking by its employees. Even if you did manage to read all of it, what are the chances that you would remember this piece of information a week from now?

The original case study had around 3000 words which were used to describe in great detail the media group, what it did, the nitty gritty of the problem and the intricacies of the architectural solution. What are the chances that you would have actually read through the entire document if I had reproduced it for you? Zero.

In fact, in most companies that I have helped with storytelling, very few people other than the creators of the case studies have actually read them in their entirety.

I am not surprised. I have always believed that case studies are the second-most boring documents produced in the business world after admin manuals.

They are cold, dry, formulaic documents extolling the virtues of a process, product or company. They are full of jargon, claims and assertions, often trying to oversell. As a result, they are difficult to read and impossible to remember.

But it doesn't have to be that way. After all, in most business-to-business (B2B) situations, it is precisely these examples of business problems which your company's product or service helped solve that subtly, yet very persuasively, showcases your solutions.

A very good way of making case studies interesting to read, easy to remember and effortless to retell is by introducing elements of a good story into them.

As discussed earlier, a story in business is a fact wrapped in context and delivered with emotion. So, we are not talking about inventing or creating stories, but using the facts we already have in our current case studies.

Now you may be wondering how a case study about your company's integrated oilfield water management solution for a petroleum firm in a developed country can have any emotion whatsoever attached to it.

Well, the person in the petroleum firm who was facing the problem surely had emotions about the problem he was facing. He may have been frustrated, anxious, burnt out and at his wits' end about the problem. He associated negative emotions with the issue.

When the team in your company, using your product and services helped solve his problem, I am sure he had an emotional response. These could be relief, satisfaction and excitement about the way forward. The success of having solved the problem, with your product's help, may have brought him recognition, accolades and rewards, which would have given him emotions of pride and inspired him to do more.

When you introduce the person at the heart of the story and tell us how he felt, you engage the readers. They connect with the protagonist and want to read on to see how this challenge was solved and how it all ended happily. All of us like happy endings. All of us like resolutions.

When we create a connection between the listener and the central character of the story, and the listener resonates with, 'Yes, I have the same problem', that is when the case study, or what we call a success story, really hits home.

Another powerful element to add is the name of the person you or your firm helped. A name helps build connection and empathy. Think of your favourite novel. Imagine if I took it back from you and replaced the name of the hero with 'the hero', 'he', 'him', 'his' and gave the book back to you. Would it be the same book?

No? Why not? After all, it is the same plot. It has the same climax. It has the same ending. The reason is that we can't empathize with 'the hero'. We empathize with human beings, and for that we need a name.

The question that arises is: What about our confidentiality clause? Sometimes, we can't disclose who the client is. The answer is: Make up a name. No, don't pretend the name is Ravi. Tell your listener that you are making up the name. You say, 'We were working with the CEO of a large supermarket chain headquartered in Hyderabad. Let's call him Ravi.' After the next few sentences, your audience will ignore the fact that the name was made up and start empathizing with Ravi, the problems Ravi faces, and the emotions Ravi feels.

Let's use these principles for the case study reproduced at the beginning of the chapter. In case you have already forgotten, it was about increasing the video-processing throughput of a media company.

There must have been a person incharge of the media group's effort to monetize their content across platforms. Let's call her Ruchira. She must have been observing how media companies across the world were making a lot of progress in monetizing content.

She must have been aware of what could be achieved if only she could process more videos every day. But the ability to do so was outside her ken, and she must have had feelings about this. She would possibly be feeling helpless and frustrated.

The team from the IT company must have been led by someone. Let's call him Rajiv. For someone to be able to think innovatively, the person must have been curious and willing to go beyond just the basic task assigned, in this case that of digital content management, and take a holistic view of the end goal—more content for viewers. Now, with these assumptions, here is how it could be rewritten.

In 2011, we were working with the business head for the digital business at a large media company. Let's call her Ruchira. Ruchira had identified a huge opportunity in monetizing the rich content that the company had. However, the content processing was slow and error-prone, and this frustrated her. She knew that this was a huge opportunity loss.

That's when Ruchira engaged us to help her with digital content management. The key task of the group, headed by Rajiv, was to index and convert the content in a way that would allow consumption across different customer platform. However, the video-processing speeds were very low. A two-GB video was taking twenty minutes to process, thus, allowing the media house to publish only seventy-two videos in a day. This was resulting in low business.

While working on processing, speed was not part of our mandate. Rajiv knew this was impacting the overall goal Ruchira had. That is when he and his team came up with an out-of-the-box solution. They suggested replacing the current single-threaded video model for video transcoding with a multithreaded one. Multithreaded execution enabled parallel processing of new and cached videos, thereby increasing the number of videos getting processed in a day and generating more business for the customer.

After Rajiv's team made this architectural change, the media house started processing over 750 two-GB videos every day, hence increasing its total business ten fold. This small idea has been generating close to $6 million of additional revenues a year. Ruchira was overjoyed with the success. This achievement was recognized by the media house as one of the top ten revenue-generating ideas of the year.

Isn't this version much more memorable than the previous one? What changed?

First, we introduced the person at the heart of the story. You will notice that the fact that Ruchira wasn't her real name did not impact your engagement with the story.

In the first version, you read about a 'media company involved in developing high-profile, lifestyle-oriented content for many media platforms including television, digital, mobile and publishing'. As you read that did you visualize anything? No. We can't visualize 'a media company', but we can all visualize Ruchira. Neither did the piece help create any empathy for the media company's problem, but you can empathize with the frustration that Ruchira had.

It is these two elements of visualization and emotion that help us remember Ruchira's story.

It is not that you need to convert your case study into a full-fledged drama. You would have noticed that the number of words used to describe Ruchira's emotions is a minuscule percentage of the entire text.

This approach of using success stories not only makes case studies interesting to read and easy to understand, but also has another huge benefit—like any other story, these are easy to remember and effortless to retell.

In a recent example, one of my clients reported that they believed that one of the key elements that helped them win a pitch was a success story. The story they had shared during the pitch was retold by one of the client employees during internal decision-making meetings. That really helped as the success story was very powerful in explaining how their product had helped other clients.

When we pitch to clients, we don't always get to meet all the decision makers. When clients have internal meetings to choose products, services and vendors, often only features and benefits of different offerings of different vendors are discussed, as the case studies we have left behind are either never read, or if read, never retold. Using a story structure makes it easy for these to be remembered and retold.

So, go ahead and recast your case studies by incorporating the client whose problem your product solved into the heart of the story, tell us how the emotional arc changed from struggle to elation, and watch us want to read your success story to the very end. And then, watch how a boring piece of document becomes a story being retold.

9

Story Listening

IT'S 7 DECEMBER 2014. Huddled in a soundproof recording booth at the Grand Central Terminal, New York, John Heyn asks his uncle, Herman Heyn, 'How did you decide to become a street corner astronomer?'

John, an ordinary American citizen, is using a booth set up by an organization called StoryCorps to record an interview that can help him understand his uncle better and later serve as a memory. StoryCorps is an American non-profit organization whose mission is to record, preserve and share the stories of Americans from all backgrounds and beliefs.

Uncle Herman started by describing how his science teacher, Miss Wicker, triggered his love for the stars. As he narrated his life journey, he said:

Well, you know, I have always had what I call an 'education bone'. I got a degree in elementary education in general science, but I decided I didn't want to teach in a classroom because of my learning disabilities. I couldn't remember kids' names. I couldn't even get organized enough to write them down.

And so I went into various kinds of jobs. Each time I'd start a new job, I'd say, 'I'm going to stay with it. I'm going to get benefits and vacation and retirement and raises.' But three years later, I wouldn't be able to stand it anymore, I had to get out of there and get another job. I had so many jobs, I can't even make a list of them, but it would be a very long list.

And then, one beautiful night in November 1987, the moon was up, Jupiter was up, and I had nothing on my schedule. And so I decided, heck, I'm going to take my telescope out on the street and invite people to look at the stars. And as I was walking out the door, I said, 'Oh, I'll take a tip hat with me, too, and see what happens.'

I set up the telescope at Fells Point, and I had people looking at the moon and Jupiter. I think that first night I made $10. Then I went back the next night and made $40, and I moved the hat a little closer. I said, 'Well, if I can make money at this, maybe I can do it full-time.'

This is a small portion of just one of the over 1,65,000 stories that StoryCorps[1] captured in the USA ever since they set up their first recording booth in the Grand Central Terminal in 2003. David Isay, the founder of StoryCorps, started his story collection when he discovered that he had made what he called 'an idiotic mistake'. He had lost the recording of an audio interview he had made years ago of his grandmother and her three sisters.

Initially, all the stories were collected in booths set up by StoryCorps across the USA. Then in 2015, he won the $1 million TED prize and used it to launch the StoryCorps app. This has now taken the story collection across the world.

In all these years of story collection, StoryCorps has developed a high level of intelligence on what elicits stories from people. The section called 'Great Questions' on the StoryCorps website is a treasure trove of powerful questions that have, time and again, helped elicit over 1,65,000 stories.

Not surprising, most of the questions can be bucketed under *when, where, who* and around *emotions. When* and *where* give us the time and location markers. *Who* reminds us of the characters. And triggering the relevant emotions brings back the memories attached to them. We remember incidences when we had those memories.

These findings are no different from the ones we have had in our journey to collect stories. But first I need to answer the question: Why collect stories?

The first reason is that if you have now been convinced of the power of stories in business, and if you have decided that you will be a storyteller, you possibly cannot be a one-story wonder. Imagine what it would be like if every time I approached a group, someone whispered, 'Oh no! IC is coming. I hope he doesn't tell us his Club Mahindra story again.'

To be an effective storyteller, we need to have a bagful of stories that we continuously refresh. There are three rich sources where we get stories from. The first, and perhaps the most powerful source, are your own stories. From the very moment we are born to now, we have been part of thousands and thousands of tiny anecdotes, some that have shaped us, our beliefs and demonstrated to the world who we really are. Many of these anecdotes can be used even in the business context.

This is my most preferred source. Here there is no question of story verification, no requirement to look for any missing details either. It is our story, and we know everything about it. These are the stories we tell most passionately. While, like any other stories, these too get across the point, they also pass on a few messages about us—what we value, what are our beliefs and who we are.

Let me give you an example. The other day, I was addressing a set of people who had recently started their first job. Among other things, I wanted to make a point that when faced with a crisis, one needs to remain calm, evaluate the options and think about a clear plan of action before jumping into execution. To drive home this point, I decided to share an experience that I had had just a week before this.

One of our dogs, a golden retriever, is traumatized by loud noise. So, last week my wife and I, in order to help him escape the tyranny of the Diwali firecrackers, took him and our pug to a farmhouse on the outskirts of Mumbai. On the day we were to come back, we suddenly realized that Zen, our golden retriever, was missing. I had seen him 10–15 minutes earlier, but now he didn't seem to be around. I was quite certain that he must be somewhere close by. But when the initial five minutes of whistling for him and calling out his name did not yield results, frenzy set in. All of us, including the seven staff members of the farmhouse, were running around the 10-acre property calling out his name. In this melee, I mentioned to one of the staff members that he should open the doors to all the garden sheds, staff quarters, garages, etc., to check whether Zen was there. Over the next forty-five minutes, we looked everywhere frantically. Just as I was about to go to the nearby village to call people and create a search party, one of the members of the cleaning staff opened an unused guest room next to the room in which we were staying, and out came Zen, wagging his tail.

When I think about this incident, the thought that he might have walked into some sort of a closed space and that the door might have shut behind him had definitely crossed my mind. However, instead of diligently following through on that thought, I had continued to run around screaming his name, to the same areas of the property that I had already been to several times. It is incidents like these that have made me believe that keeping a calm head during a crisis and thinking through possible options before taking action will always be more productive.

I'm sure that you can see how sharing this incident, along with my opinion, would have had a more powerful impact on my audience compared to simply sharing my wisdom.

The second source is stories other people tell us. Now that you understand the ingredients that make up a story, your story antenna has been activated. You will be able to spot stories a mile away. If someone starts with a time or location marker, for example, 'A few months ago . . .', your story antenna should go up. And then, if you find the story powerful, it's one more for your collection.

The third source is business books. Almost all business books you have read in the past have multiple stories. It's just that you weren't actively looking for them. Now you will. Try this—reread any one of your favourite business books, and you will find that it is full of little anecdotes, author's experiences and examples to illustrate points the author is making. All stories. It doesn't have to be a biography. Any business book will do.

While all the three sources are rich, perhaps the richest source of stories that is most relevant for your business is each and every employee, each partner and indeed each stakeholder. The only challenge is that you will not be able to get them to tell you a story by asking the simple question: 'Can you tell me a story about . . .'

A question like that will get you nowhere. While the direct question will not work, there are a few simple ways in which we can get people to tell us stories. All of them revolve around being able to take the listener back to a moment in their lives. When our minds are taken back to any particular moment, we remember the experience. There are three ways to do so.

The first way to get a story is to tell a story. I am sure that you would have noticed several instances when, listening to someone else tell a story, you have remembered stories of your own. And, of course, you were dying to share them. That is essentially how we have conversations. Others tell us about their experiences, we listen to them. Acknowledge their feelings, ask a few questions and then share your own experience. Listening to a story often takes us back to a moment in time where we had the same or similar experience. Someone shares with us about how he or she was disappointed when she visited a restaurant that was his or her childhood favourite only to find that the food did not have the same mouth-watering taste he or she remembers. Immediately, we, as the listener, remember the time when we had a similar experience.

The second way involves asking the right questions. When we first learnt to speak, our favourite question was *why*. As we started working, a question hierarchy was drilled into our head. Of the four w's and one h, clearly *why* was the most important question, followed by *what* and *how*. *When* and *where* are at the bottom of that hierarchy.

This hierarchy doesn't work when we are collecting stories. The top three questions—*why*, *what* and *how*—are opinion-generating questions. They don't get people back to any moment in time and hence can't get us a story. Try it out. Ask any question beginning with any one of these three and you will see that you get an opinion.

But asking the *when* and *where* questions usually allow us to take the other person back to a moment in time. As you would have figured, *when* gives us the time marker and *where* gives us a location marker, two elements that we discussed in Chapter 2 are the critical ingredients of stories.

The third way to get people to remember stories is to use emotion words in a question. This needs a bit of preparation. Ask yourself what emotions might the other person have gone through around the subject on which you are looking for a story. Let's say you are looking for a few stories on innovation that the person would have either observed or been a part of. The emotions the person might have gone through when they were successful with an innovation could have been pride, joy, excitement, surprise, appreciation, etc. Now that you have identified these words, you can ask questions like: 'can you remember a time when you felt very proud of a breakthrough you had?' or 'when was the last time you were really excited on discovering a new approach?'

Most of our memory is stored in our brain with an emotional charge. My experience with running anecdote circles (group discussions designed to elicit stories) has shown that when we can trigger an emotion, the likelihood of getting a story is higher. There is a science behind this as well. Other than the existence of chemical Post-it notes that I described in Chapter 1, researchers have also discovered that surges of the stress hormone, norepinephrine (also known as noradrenaline), that often accompany strong emotions spark a series of molecular events that ultimately strengthen the connections between neurons.[2] The strength of the connection determines the longevity of the memory.

Using these three approaches usually gets us a story. However, all is not lost if we have heard an opinion. We just need to probe further. Let's assume we asked, 'tell me about a time you were really excited about discovering a new approach', and the person answers, 'I am always excited when I discover new approaches.' We need to then press on for a specific instance: 'Can you tell me about the last time it happened?'

While one of the reasons for collecting stories is to build our collection, story listening (along with storytelling) can be used in multiple other interventions like managing change, embedding values, managing knowledge, probing the underlying reason for certain employee behaviours, etc. We will talk about some of them in the following chapters.

PART III

Putting Them Together

10

Getting Values to Be Understood, Remembered and Put into Action

I N THIS PART of the book we will start putting the tools and techniques we learnt in Part II to use. We will identify some of the critical challenges we face in business and apply the various techniques—storytelling and story listening—to address them.

'What is transparency?' I asked.

He said, 'A value'.

'Tell me more.'

'It is the most important value for our organization.'

'What do you do in this organization? What is your role?'

'I am a medical representative. I meet doctors in order to promote our products. I do this by giving them product awareness, answering their queries, providing advice and introducing products.'

'Give me an example of an instance where you think you had displayed this value, lived this value.'

He thought for a while, his eyes rolled to the top left corner as he struggled to retrieve a memory. Then his eyes lit up, he smiled and said, 'Yes. It was in the middle of last year. Around August. We had had a price increase across our portfolio, and I had stayed up till very late to ensure that I sent WhatsApp messages to all my doctors about the price increase. I think that is a demonstration of our value of transparency.'

This medical representative wasn't pulling my leg. He genuinely thought that what he had described was a display of transparency. Technically, he was correct. If he had actively tried to keep the information from the doctors, clearly he wouldn't have been behaving transparently. But that is certainly not what the company had in mind when it articulated that as a value.

This conversation happened during a consulting project I was running for a global pharmaceutical giant. Let us call it Agile Innovative Pharmaceuticals (AIP).

AIP's head office was concerned that employees across the world did not have a shared understanding of what their five values—client-centricity, courage, transparency, solidarity, collaboration—really meant.

In order to ensure a uniform understanding and adherence to these core values, AIP had set up a central committee—Ethics and Values Oversight Committee. This committee had engaged a global market research agency to determine the current state of affairs, and the report was not very encouraging. The knowledge of what the five values were varied across geographies. In the country where the employees' recalling of the five values was the highest, the score stood at 64 per cent. That is, 64 per cent of the employees could correctly recall what the five values were. The lowest score for any country was 22 per cent. And even in the country with the highest recall, very few people had the same understanding of what those values really meant or what those values looked like in action.

But this finding is not surprising at all. Unless your organization is a complete outlier, I am reasonably sure the state of affairs is not very different. In most organizations, values end up being a plaque on the wall behind the reception, or on the wall of the boardroom or the wall of the chairman's office.

It is not that organizations don't think awareness and complete understanding of the core values are not important. Most of them make a lot of effort during the induction process. Many create manuals and books explaining what these mean. But all this rarely works. That is because words like client-centricity, courage, transparency, solidarity, collaboration are abstract. As we discussed in Chapter 1, when we hear an abstract word we don't understand, our brain doesn't instruct us to ask for an explanation. It just makes it up. As a result, different employees have a different understanding of the same word. Writing down explanations is not a very useful way as it is usually more English words explaining an abstract word.

The way to create concreteness instead of abstraction is to share stories about these values in action. In the stories, these values are being demonstrated by colleagues, leaders, peers and juniors. So, instead of spending hours trying to define what these terms mean, we help people work it out for themselves by giving them examples of the values being lived within the organization. You might remember that I mentioned in the introductory chapter that how as a chief marketing officer at Mahindra Holidays I struggled to embed values and how using stories moved us from failure to success. Just as an aside—you do remember the story of the receptionist at the Coorg resort of Mahindra Holidays, right?

Well, that is the power of stories.

And that is what I had proposed AIP do. They agreed, and I started working on the project.

One day, as part of this project, I had gathered about ten medical representatives from across AIP's various businesses. We were assembled in a small conference room in one of their regional offices.

I wanted to know what their understanding of the five AIP values—client-centricity, courage, transparency, solidarity, collaboration—was. In order to do that, I wanted them to tell me stories about situations or moments when they had seen these values being displayed by either their colleagues or themselves.

I was doing some story listening, running what we call an anecdote circle.

A lot of steps had been undertaken before this event. A core team at AIP and I had worked on how many such groups we would run. This was based on trying to get as much representation as possible from various levels of the field force, gender, geography and lines of business. The selected participants were sent an invitation letter explaining the objectives of the session.

I had arrived a few hours earlier, armed with a voice recorder to record the stories, a list of story-eliciting questions we had put together (based on the principles shared in the chapter on story listening) and a few stories of people in other organizations displaying these values. I had also made sure that I was using the vocabulary of the organization. Every corporate tribe has a language replete with three-letter acronyms. Using the language they know is a good way to make them feel that you have taken the effort to understand them.

I have seen that stories flow better when the physical space we use is a warm and friendly environment. My favourite is to find one of those new-age meeting places where you have various choices of seating—I love bean bags. However, this was not possible in this case, so we were using a regular conference room. But we ensured that everyone would be seated in a circle—an indication that we were all equal and giving me a chance to be treated as a fellow storyteller and not a facilitator.

As agreed with the AIP core team, they had organized some tea and snacks—it is amazing how good a story lubricator food is. It is another great step towards creating a warm environment.

My initial thought was to allow free-seating and have the participants sit where they wanted. But, just in time, I remembered an advice Shawn and Mark from Anecdote had given me based on their years of experience. They had said 'try and find out in advance whether there are people in the group who dominate and talk non-stop. Make them sit beside you. When they sit opposite you they will keep having eye contact and feel encouraged to keep talking. When they face away, it seems to reduce their desire to speak.' Such good advice to remember. I quickly spoke to the AIP core team and marked out the seating accordingly.

After the participants filed in and took their places, I introduced myself and explained the reason why we had gathered here.

I avoid the use of the word 'story' in the initial portion of the discussion as there is a high chance that most of them wouldn't have been exposed to the ideas we are discussing in this book. They might start thinking of what they would have to creatively make up. So, I use the word 'experience'. I say something like, 'Today I would like to listen to your experiences, incidences where either you, your colleagues or your leaders have lived these values.'

Then on a whiteboard or chart paper I write, 'I think . . .' I ask the participants whether most of the conversations they have had in conference rooms began with these two words. They all say, 'Yes!'

I then strike through these two words and write 'I remember . . .'

I say, 'For today, it would be great if you can consciously avoid sentences which begin with "I think" and craft sentences that begin with "I remember".'

I then share a few guidelines. The first, of course, is to share examples and experiences. The second is to not interrupt each other. The third is to not disagree when a colleague describes an event, but to say 'I had a different experience' and then share that.

Now, coming back to the group I was with that morning. Taking the value—transparency—as the first subject, I asked: 'Think about a time when you saw someone in this organization display transparency.' I then sat back and waited. Almost always there is silence. I have learnt to live with it and control the urge to speak. I leave that to someone else in the group. Very soon, someone says, 'Okay, I'll go first . . .' and the story collection begins.

As the discussions continue, there will be participants who veer into an opinion such as 'I think the team from the vaccines business are always living these values. They are always transparent.' It is now my turn to jump in and ask, 'Can you give me an example? When was the last time you saw this happening?' My job is to steer them back to stories.

Think back on all the focus group discussions you would have attended at work, and think of how often the facilitator speaks. Didn't most facilitators almost always have something to say after any of the participants spoke? It is rare in a focus group for the facilitator to keep silent and let the participants keep discussing among themselves. But it is key when running an anecdote circle. The facilitator recedes to the background and lets the participants tell stories. Stories trigger stories, and I let that happen. I only jump in when someone violates the guidelines, or shares what I think is an opinion, or when someone goes off-track and shares experiences not related to the subject being discussed.

Sometimes, a group falls silent. That is a good time for me to tell a story from the ones I had selected as part of my preparation. In the first group in a project it is usually a story from my experience or something I had heard or read where someone was displaying the behaviour. In subsequent groups, I invariably have stories to share from the same organization.

These are the ones I have heard in previous groups. This story sharing is again to trigger stories. I am sure you have observed this phenomenon while you were reading this book. Many stories I shared would have reminded you of similar stories you know.

A lot of stories I hear in such groups are clearly not a demonstration of what the company had in mind when they chose that value. For example, at AIP, I heard of WhatsApp messaging about a price increase, which I shared earlier. Another example was this incident: 'The new product manager really believes in transparency. Most of the previous product managers I have worked with used very high-level English words. Coming from Bengali-medium schools, my colleagues and I often didn't know those words and struggled to understand the meaning of the sentences in the product detailing meetings. The new product manager uses simple words that everybody understands. This is very good. He is displaying a lot of transparency.'

However, among all this 'junk' are 'jewels' like the incident below, which was narrated to me by a participant in Mumbai. He had just been promoted and had moved from a suburban town to Mumbai.

This happened when I was stationed in Malegaon in 2012. I rarely met my targets those days as they were very tough. Then, suddenly, in the month of May, I actually overshot my target. The sale of a product called Heal-Ear (name changed in order to provide anonymity) was the cause for this. That was very surprising as Heal-Ear is a speciality drug which is supposed to be used by ENT surgeons for post-operative care. Malegaon didn't have an ENT specialist, let alone an ENT surgeon. I couldn't think of any reason behind the sales shooting up. I started investigating.

After tracing the sales through three stockists, we zeroed-in on the doctor who was prescribing this. He wasn't an ENT specialist, and we had never met him before. The facts he shared shocked me.

A few months ago, he had a patient who came in with a complaint of severe pain in the ear. Regular antibiotics didn't seem to solve the problem, and so the local doctor referred the patient to renowned ENT surgeon Dr Ismail Ansari who had a clinic in Mumbai. Dr Ansari did the operation and prescribed Heal-Ear for post-operative care. When the patient went back and showed the prescription to the local doctor, the doctor started prescribing Heal-Ear for all patients with similar problems. We asked him to stop this immediately and explained to him what this drug was for. We, of course, saw our sales plummet in June, but this is something we would always do when faced with such a situation.

What a powerful example of living the value—transparency.

Now, when stories like this are communicated across the organization, people start to get a shared and common understanding of what the value looks like in action.

So, this is how one takes something abstract like values and embeds it across the organization.

The full process has three phases:

1. Collecting and selecting stories.
2. Broadcasting the stories and recognizing the heroes.
3. Creating a sustainable cycle.

Let me explain these in more detail.

Collecting and Selecting Stories

This is where we do the initial story collection by running anecdote circles, like I shared in the example above. We do this by using the techniques explained in the previous chapter on story listening.

We need to be prepared that a large percentage of stories in this phase would be unusable because most of the employees are yet to have a shared and correct understanding of what the values look like in action. But like I said earlier, among all the junk, you will find jewels—like the Club Mahindra story about the receptionist in Coorg living the value of 'no room for ordinary', or the AIP story about the medical representative living the value of 'transparency'.

Having collected and selected the stories that really demonstrate the values, we move to the second phase.

Broadcasting the Stories and Recognizing the Heroes

In this phase, we use one of two approaches. One approach is to get the senior leadership (CEO included) to share the story. Starting with, 'I just heard about Ravi. Ravi is the receptionist at our Coorg resort . . .' and ending with 'what a great demonstration of how to live the value—no room for ordinary.' The second approach is to get the protagonist to tell the story.

Of course, getting the storyteller to understand the essential story elements is a good idea. You will remember these were shared in Chapter 3—time/location, sequence of causal events, character and surprise ending.

I am a big believer in the power of oral storytelling rather than the written word and hence always recommend that these stories are told. Also, videos are so much easier to consume than the written word. Besides, the cost and availability of high bandwidth is no longer a concern.

You don't need to get into a professional video shoot for this. Talking into a good phone camera will work. You can share this video with the entire employee base using a YouTube video channel, hosted on the company intranet site, Yammer, Facebook or the all-pervasive WhatsApp groups.

Having the senior leaders narrate the story is powerful recognition. In addition, senior leaders narrating stories indicate that values are really important for the organization and not just posters and plaques created by the human resources department.

Creating a Sustainable Cycle

This is the hard part, but it is more than worth it.

This phase involves setting up a process by which we are continuously collecting, selecting and broadcasting stories on a cyclical basis. The hurdles we need to cross are two: inertia and the difference between orality and literacy. Inertia of adding any new element to an already overflowing checklist makes regular and voluntary sharing of stories a bothersome task for employees. In my experience, it initially needs to come as a mandate. The best way to get started is a diktat from the top.

Every team needs to send a minimum number of stories for each value every month—I am usually good with one or two per team. Teams can be demarcated by location, function or business unit or a combination of these, e.g., the eastern region sales team.

Just a mandate isn't enough. Urgent work has a tendency to overtake important work. Often, building cultural elements like values, etc., are accorded lower priority than meeting this month's target. So, it is essential to have a dedicated person working under the aegis of the CEO's office who tracks, reports progress and highlights non-adherence. This is required for the first few months till the system runs smoothly.

This resource attached to the CEO's office is also responsible for getting a core group to read the stories collected every month and select the best one for each value. The selected stories are sent back to the teams. Again, the mandate is that every monthly meeting across the organization must start with sharing the best story for each value. Each of these stories are usually not more than two minutes long. With four values it is an item that takes less than ten minutes of the meeting but is a great investment.

Some organizations have a large number of values on their list. In this case, my recommendation is to choose three or four values to drive every quarter. The system will collapse if teams need to collect stories for eight or nine values and if every team meeting needs to start with sharing eight or nine stories.

As multiple stories are shared, the employees' understanding of the behaviours expected for each value become more and more concrete.

There is also an additional benefit of this process. As the process rolls on, if one sees that for a certain value no pertinent stories are coming in, there is clearly a bottleneck somewhere.

It is time to go and listen to the employees again. This time, it is to collect stories about incidences where they have seen employees fail to live these values. Then we need to make sense of patterns that emerge and take remedial measures. An example of this was when I was doing such a project for a large insurance company. One of their values was 'agility'. Agility was about quick turnaround time for both insurance policy applications as well as settlements.

While the company was getting a lot of stories for other values, there were hardly any stories on agility. When they went back to the employees and collected stories about the barriers to agility, a pattern emerged. What the employees shared was that it was very difficult to display this value when one of the key deliverables of their job was adherence to the multiple processes and levels of authorization. Once this was identified, the processes were simplified without losing the rigour, levels of authorization reduced and empowerment increased at all levels. Then, stories on agility started to flow.

One organization that has been using this process for decades, and has almost taken it to a fine art, is The Ritz-Carlton Hotel Company.[1] This hotel chain is known for exemplary customer service. It does not manage to continuously deliver this by merely training employees about the things they must do or things they must avoid. That list would be endless. Instead, they have built a story-based programme that instils a customer service ethic in all their employees. This is how it works.

Everyone in the company from around the world is encouraged to submit stories about the Ritz-Carlton people going above and beyond. Each week, a story is selected and sent out to all Ritz-Carlton hotels. It is read out at the line-up meetings when the staff gathers before starting a shift. The Ritz-Carlton calls them 'wow' stories.

Three times a week, on Mondays, Wednesdays and Fridays, the staff recounts 'wow' stories in the line-ups. Each time such a story is told, it triggers a conversation about what everyone sees as significant in it and often prompts the retelling of other stories about things that have happened in their own hotel. So, rather than receiving a corporate directive on how to behave, the staff vicariously experiences behaviours that everyone recognizes as exemplary.

At the end of the year, there is a competition to select the top ten stories.

This process of replacing abstraction with concreteness works powerfully in many other areas as well—making sense of customer feedback, understanding the drivers of employee engagement, and external sharing of the values and beliefs of the organization as it builds the employer brand.

Let's discuss some of them in the subsequent chapters.

11

Understanding Complex Human Issues by Listening to Stories

SUJIT NAIR WAS perplexed. Last year, the global consulting firm he worked for had invested a considerable amount in measuring employee engagement. The survey had helped the firm identify four areas that offered potential for improvement. It told them that these areas were important to their people, but it didn't tell them what was driving the low scores, or what they could focus on to improve them. The areas that got low scores were: 'this is a psychologically and emotionally healthy place to work in', 'we have special and unique benefits here', 'appraisals in this company are fair', and 'I feel I make a difference here.'

Sujit was asked to head a cross-functional team to understand one of the areas that got a low score: 'appraisals in this company are fair.' His team would then need to design interventions to correct the situation. The team had brainstormed and come up with a few hypotheses. This was followed by surveys and group discussions to confirm or reject the individual hypothesis. Recommendations based on the results were presented to the senior leadership. Some recommendations were accepted and interventions put into action. The survey was repeated this year and the scores dipped further. Sujit was clueless. What had gone wrong?

Over the last few years, my own work has convinced me that such problems occur because we try to solve human issues with approaches better used to solve problems with machines or markets. The flawed assumption is that even in organizational behaviour, a certain level of predictability and order exists.

The Cynefin (pronounced cun-ev-in) framework throws light on this problem. Developed by David Snowden in 1999,[1] it is based on concepts of knowledge management and organizational strategy. Snowden argues that most problems we face in business can be categorized into four parts: simple, complicated, complex and chaotic. In simple and complicated problems, causality is easy to establish either by categorizing or analysing. With complex problems the cause and effect relationship is so intertwined that things only make sense in hindsight. There is no single correct answer. The way to make progress here is to sense the patterns.

Areas like culture, innovation, leadership, trust—all messy 'people' things fall into this quadrant.

Chaotic problems are those where categorizing, analysing or sensing doesn't work. The variables are so many that cause and effect have no perceivable relationship.

What interests me in this framework is the complex quadrant, which deals with people. It requires us to recognize patterns and make sense of the issue. This is where stories come in handy. Stories have always helped us make sense of the world around us. By collecting stories using the story-listening technique and then looking at patterns that emerge can help us make sense of complex human issues at work. Let me use two case studies to illustrate this.

Employee Engagement in a Global Consulting Firm

Let's get back to Sujit Nair's problem. The low score that Sujit was trying to impact was on 'fairness in appraisal'.

Let's look at what Sujit and his team did and what may have been the lacunae in each step. The steps they took were: brainstorm for a hypothesis, conduct a survey to accept or reject this hypothesis, and recommend interventions based on the result.

This process assumes that his team was able to generate a mutually exclusive and collectively exhaustive list of hypotheses. It also assumes that any subsequent survey or group discussion to test these hypotheses will generate responses that are a true reflection of reality and not a bunch of opinions. Both these assumptions are flawed. The knowledge of the team would have constrained the variety of hypothesis generated by the brainstorm. This knowledge cannot be exhaustive. And opinions voiced by the respondents in the research would always be coloured by socially acceptable answers and group thinking.

So, after two consecutive years of low scores, the management agreed to use the story approach.

We used anecdote circles to collect stories about appraisals from employees across the company. As described in Chapter 9, we asked questions like: Tell us about your experience with appraisals in the company, tell us when was the last time you felt happy or frustrated with the appraisal? What happened? After the first group, we shared a few stories to trigger more stories.

After the stories were collected and cleaned up, we ran a workshop we call 'sense making and intervention design'. At the start of the workshop, the participants—senior management who could take decisions—were asked to read all the stories we had put up on the wall. We asked them to look at patterns that might have emerged. Remember in the discussion about the Cynefin framework we discussed that people issues are complex and that the processes that need to be used are 'probe', 'sense' and 'respond'. The probe was the story collection. This workshop was about the next two steps.

When we ask participants in such workshops to read the stories in silence and note their observations down, I can almost hear the proverbial penny drop.

In this company, the senior management discovered a few patterns. One such pattern was that employees felt that the appraisal discussions were not authentic, that they were just a formality ticked off the list. The discussion had no bearing on the appraisal as the appraisers had already made up their mind. One of the stories in this pattern went like this:

I don't think appraisals in this company are fair. Last year, when my appraisal was being done, my boss answered a few SMSs. Once his laptop pinged and he looked at it and said, 'This is important. Give me a moment,' and answered that email. Even before the end of the discussion, he looked over my shoulder, waved at someone and said, 'Get a cup of coffee, I am coming.' I think everything is pre-decided, and these discussions are a sham.

The beauty of this approach is that we are pretty good at pattern recognition. Once the pattern is recognized, designing an intervention is easy.

In this case, the team decided that they would do two interventions. One, the appraisers would be taken through a workshop on appreciative inquiry. Second, appraisal zones would be created where appraisers would go armed with only a printed appraisal and a pen, without any gadgets, and focus on the discussion. The HR department would ensure that these appraisals would only be accepted when the discussion summary was noted on the appraisal sheet and signed by both the appraiser and the appraisee. These interventions made a huge impact and the scores shot up the following year.

Using Stories to Understand Culture Transformation

Most attempts to drive cultural transformation in organizations happen when a company is looking for a dramatic shift in its business outcomes. Perhaps there has been a merger or acquisition, and it is important that the investment is fruitful. Or perhaps a new CEO has been appointed with a mandate to turn around the company.

Changing an organization's culture is one of the most difficult leadership challenges. That's because an organization's culture comprises an interlocking set of goals, roles, processes, values, communication practices, attitudes and assumptions.

These elements also impact each other.

Imagine the organization wants to promote a new behaviour, which they believe will drive positive outcomes for the organization. A team was set up to drive this initiative and they have completed a pilot intervention, and they need to know if it was successful. It's success would determine a cross-company rollout.

Given that employee behaviour is impacted by several cultural elements described above, how does the team ascertain whether the initiative has actually worked?

How does the team find out whether the new behaviour is triggered by the initiative or by something else? Is the business impact because of this new behaviour or because of some other element? There are too many causal links. This is a typical problem that would fall in David Snowden's complex domain described above.

This is where an approach based on story collection can be very powerful. One such approach is called the Most Significant Change (MSC) technique.

In the 1990s, a US-based NGO was running a programme in Bangladesh that required the villagers' participation. Spread over ten districts with 785 villages, it involved 46,000 people. Nearly 80 per cent of the direct beneficiaries were women. Various forms of development assistance like skill training, microfinancing and grants were being provided.

Monitoring the process and outcome of such a large-scale project, that too with activities which were open-ended, was a major problem.

So, in 1994, Rick Davies developed the MSC technique as part of his PhD associated with monitoring and evaluation. His aim was to evaluate the impact of the project in the Rajshahi zone of western Bangladesh. The project in this area had 140 NGO staff and covered approximately 16,500 people grouped into 503 *shomitis* (associations).

There were many stakeholders—the donors from the USA, the NGO staff in the Dhaka head office, the NGO staff in Rajshahi, the shomitis and their members.

Like different stakeholders wear different lenses in commercial organizations, the stakeholders in this project too had diverse and conflicting views of what needed to be measured. Rick gave up the attempt to get everyone to agree on a set of indicators. Instead, he collected stories from both the NGO staff and shomiti members, who were the ultimate beneficiaries, about any significant change they had seen as a result of the project. The storytellers were also asked to explain why they thought the change described in their story was significant.

A participatory approach to monitoring and evaluation was used. In order to get all stakeholders involved and appreciate the impact of the project, Rick ensured that the story selection was done at different levels of the project hierarchy. Each group had to also explain why the change stories they chose were the most significant. This approach systematically developed an intuitive and aligned understanding of the project's impact that could be communicated in conjunction with hard facts.

Rick's approach was highly successful. Because all stakeholders were involved in monitoring and evaluation, the participation increased, and so did the impact. Over the last two decades, MSC technique has been used in evaluating several NGO projects across the world. It is now slowly being accepted and adopted by commercial organizations as well.

So, when studying the impact of culture transformation initiatives within the organization, this same process of story collection and using the patterns that the stories portray can be used very powerfully.

These were two examples of how story listening can help us understand complex human issues better.

Other Powerful Uses of Story Listening

'THAT'S ONE SMALL step for a man, one giant leap for mankind,' said Neil Armstrong on 20 July 1969.

Over the next few years, eleven other astronauts landed on the moon and got back to earth. Certainly no mean feat then and no mean feat even now.

But can it happen again? Why is it that we haven't had humans back on the moon since 1972? David W. DeLong in his book, *Lost Knowledge: Confronting the Threat of an Aging Workforce*,[1] has a very surprising answer—NASA no longer knows how to! He writes:

> That's because sometime in the 1990s NASA lost the knowledge it had developed to send astronauts to the moon. In an era of cost-cutting and downsizing, the engineers who designed the huge Saturn five rockets used to launch the lunar landing craft were encouraged to take early retirement

from the space programme. With them went years of experience and expertise about the design trade-offs that had been made in building the Saturn rockets. Also lost were what appears to be the last set of critical blueprints for the Saturn booster, which was the only rocket ever built with enough thrust to launch manned lunar payload.

Wow! Can you believe that?

Do you know whether parts of your organization are reinventing the wheel, not learning from past experiences or making repeated mistakes?

Well, if your organization is even a few years old, this must be happening unless you put in place a robust knowledge management practice. Managers leaving or moving to new assignments always take valuable knowledge with them. This is not because of malice but because they just don't know how much they know that the company would need. Neither does the company.

In 2004, a study of 240 organizations in the USA found that the greatest impact of employee turnover was lost knowledge, not profitability![2] Even in a country where knowledge management practices have been around, lost knowledge had negatively affected a staggering 78 per cent of the organizations.

Lost knowledge is a concern for even companies that have a detailed handover process. Why so?

There are two kinds of knowledge each of us carry about our jobs: explicit and tacit. Explicit knowledge is the 'know-what' of an organization—knowledge that can be communicated using formalized language. Tacit knowledge is the 'know-how'—knowledge that is deeply rooted in an individual's actions and experiences, as well as in the ideals, values or emotions that the person embraces.[3]

Explicit knowledge is what we can put down in a detailed handover note or express in handover discussions. Tacit knowledge is what we unknowingly carry with us when we leave a position or an organization.

Using stories is one of the more powerful knowledge management practices. Stories transform tacit knowledge into explicit knowledge and these become a great vehicle to share that knowledge.

Here is how we do it.

Knowledge Management

The first step is to identify the areas in which the person leaving a position has tacit knowledge. This is done by talking to his or her seniors, colleagues and juniors. Ask questions like: 'What are the occasions when you miss his presence the most?' or 'What kind of problems do you know he will have the solutions for?' Some of the questions you could ask the person himself or herself are: 'What have been some of the failures or failed projects during your tenure, and what have you learnt from them?' or 'What are the things you wish you knew about this job when you started?' Having identified the areas, you now need to get the person to tell you stories about these areas.

Once you have finished the story-listening session, you need to transcribe your recording, and from the transcriptions cull out and clean up the stories.

The best way to share these stories is orally. Since the person concerned would not be available forever, a good way to store these stories are through video or audio recordings. This recording has to be done separately from the first story-listening session. When people tell stories for the first time they are not always sharp and to the point. In the first telling of the story, sometimes people add information as they go along. For example, 'Oh! This happened in 1972', or 'The scientist I spoke about earlier, I remember his name now—Jaydeep Malhotra.' So, once the stories from the first round of story listening are chosen, they need to be cleaned up and organized. Then we go back to the storyteller with a video recorder and ask them to retell the polished story.

These recordings, when indexed and made available to the employees of the company and the successor of this person, become a fantastic way of retaining knowledge.

Today, NASA's Academy of Program and Project Leadership (APPL) uses storytelling as a primary vehicle for transferring project management expertise. This is done using a series of story-based knowledge-sharing meetings that are supplemented by ASK, a bimonthly online magazine. ASK is dedicated to stories about project management at NASA.

Many other organizations across the world such as the World Bank, IBM, Corning and Shell are using storytelling to capture, store and transfer knowledge.

There are several other uses of story listening, which are described below.

Building the Employer Brand

Imagine this is 1992, you are a second-year MBA student, and you have just received a five-page letter from a friend who is a batch senior to you. Your friend has just spent the first two months of an eighteen-month training programme at a leading FMCG company in the country. A few excerpts from the letter read like this:

> ... places that cannot be covered by direct distribution, e.g., small villages are covered by cinema vans. These vans are used as propaganda vehicles in order to increase awareness about our products. I have been working with one such van since yesterday. The villages we have covered are over 100 km away from Gorakhpur. During the day, we went to two villages where we set up stalls and used a loudspeaker to run ad jingles. We then stopped for lunch under a tree and the driver and helper cooked lunch. This evening, like yesterday, we plan to set up a screen in one of the villages where we will be showing a Chitrahar-type episode interspersed with our ads. All this is such a fantastic experience ...
>
> ... last two weeks were very strenuous because after returning from a full day at the market, my trainers came to the hotel and took classroom courses every day till midnight. On two days, the sessions went on till about 3.30–4 a.m. Now I know why this training programme is so famous. The amount of time my trainers are willing to spend on me (for no benefit of their own) is incredible. This is definitely not a job. I have really enrolled myself in a school of marketing funded by soaps and detergents ...[4]

Now imagine that a few days later a competing company visits the campus for a pre-placement talk. Some very senior managers in natty suits make a presentation. They start with telling you about the vision, mission and values of the company. They share last year's results and the next five years' plan to become the fastest-growing FMCG company in India. They also talk about the fact that they have brought their best global practices for trainee induction into the programme they have designed for India. They assert that the induction programme is very well designed and that the foundation they built for field sales and marketing is second to none. They finish by reminding you that in your marketing bible written by Philip Kotler, no other company has as many mentions as they have.

You now have a choice to make. Will you apply for a job in the company your senior works for (the one who wrote the letter) or the competitor?

Assertions like 'we have the best induction programme' or 'in the next five years we will be the fastest growing company' aren't often credible and can never connect to the core of an individual. Stories do. Hearing a story is as close as the listener can get to a first-hand experience. The conclusion that the listener draws for himself or herself is almost unshakeable and far more powerful than the assertions. And hence, in the above example, you would probably choose the first company.

Many companies have understood that employee speak is a powerful way to convey a message to both prospective employees and to the current employees to cement their beliefs about the company. But what most of these companies are getting wrong is that employees asserting that 'the company listens to us', 'the company empowers us from the very start', 'the company has an open culture and our bosses are very approachable' might get the listener to be sceptical about these statements. Instead, when employees tell stories about their experience of the same, the listeners draw conclusions about empowerment, approachability and all other attributes the stories display.

The best way to build the employer brand is a story at a time.

Understanding Customers/Consumers

I really rue the fact that in the two decades I spent in the field of marketing, I did not know about story listening.

My formative years in marketing were spent in Unilever, where the importance of meeting and listening to consumers was ingrained in me. While this meant that I did countless home visits and spoke to hundreds of consumers, I wonder if I truly listened. Was I really uncovering new insights or was I largely validating the hypotheses that I had? I don't think I went with a clean slate and a beginner's curiosity. I usually had either verbalized or unverbalized hypotheses, and my cognitive bias ensured that I largely listened to what I wanted to hear. I listened to whether the consumer was validating or rejecting my hypotheses and subconsciously filtered out new information. Using leading questions did not help. I was like Shakespeare's *Hamlet*. In Act III, Scene 2, Prince Hamlet is 'interviewing' Polonius, a courtier. The interaction went like this:

> Hamlet: Do you see yonder cloud that's almost in shape
> of a camel?
> Polonius: By the mass, and 'tis like a camel indeed.

Hamlet: Methinks it is like a weasel.

Polonius: It is back'd like a weasel.

Hamlet: Or like a whale?

Polonius: Very like a whale.

While Hamlet was measuring Polonius's trustworthiness or lack of it, this would be a disaster if he was truly interested in finding out what Polonius actually thought. There have been several times when I was guilty of asking such leading questions in my desire to prove my hypotheses.

As we discussed in the previous chapter, in the example of trying to understand why employees had given a low score on 'fairness in appraisals', the usual questions that start with 'why?' or 'what?' result in eliciting opinions and socially acceptable answers, which are not necessarily a true reflection of reality.

Using a story-listening approach in consumer interviews has four benefits. First, it helps redress the inherent power differential that exists between you, the big company executive, and the consumer. While a big company executive may be seen to be more knowledgeable than the consumer in many areas, there is no one better to recollect and share the experience the consumer had than the consumer himself or herself. Second, getting consumers to tell stories eases the tension the consumer often feels to provide the 'correct' or socially acceptable answer. Third, by asking the consumer to explain the meanings they attach to their experiences, one can truly get new understanding about the subject. Fourth, when one collects multiple stories, and patterns emerge, they lead to new insights. Gary Klein, the cognitive psychologist, had put it very well: 'Insight is when you unexpectedly come to a better story.'[5]

If I were to go back in time and advise the brand manager that I was in the mid-1990s, I would tell him to learn the art of story listening. Then I would go to consumers and get them to share their experiences and stories around the subject I was interested in. And then back in the office, I would look at all the stories from all the consumers I visited and make sense of any pattern that might surface. From those patterns would emerge insights.

Finding Anti-Stories

In Chapter 7, we discussed anti-stories—stories that the recipients of messages about change would have in their heads as to why the change would not work. We talked about identifying anti-stories and addressing them within the change narrative.

When trying to identify anti-stories that might exist, it is obviously not an option to say, 'Next week, the HR director is going to announce a new performance evaluation system. What are your views?' So, we conduct story-listening exercises and, from the stories we collect, see if there are any anti-story patterns.

The first step is to identify the key themes around which the strategy or change message is built. Then, for each of these themes, we would collect stories people have—both what works and what doesn't work. Then, studying the patterns that emerge from these stories, we identify the anti-stories that might exist.

In one particular change exercise, I was helping an HR director communicate the 'people policy' for the next five years. The key themes were around dramatic increase in training investments, aligning the annual bonuses around shared business goals, a new process for annual appraisal, and related bonuses and promotions. I conducted anecdote circles around these themes. While collecting stories about annual performance appraisals, I heard stories about biases, about how appraisals had been used as a way to downsize teams, about how when the current process of annual appraisals was rolled out, the annual increase in salary was negligible.

When I discussed these with the HR team, I was told that many of these were misconceptions. The slowdown of salary increment at the same time as the introduction of the current appraisals process was merely a coincidence.

Now, imagine an off-site where the HR director unveils the new strategy. An hour-long speech covers a lot of ground. He talks about the recent achievements, then lays out the next five years' HR road map, and then unveils the plan for the next year: an increased focus on training, annual bonuses to be linked to overall business performance in addition to individual performance, and the introduction of a new system to manage annual appraisals and rewards. He also adds that this new system has been designed in conjunction with an international HR consulting firm. However, in this speech, he does nothing to address the anti-stories. After the speech, there is a coffee break. What do you think happens now?

A few people gather around the foyer drinking coffee when someone says, 'Huh! The Diro is talking about how the new process to manage appraisals will ensure fair and accurate evaluation. Do you remember how our annual increase in salary almost stopped when the last one was rolled out a few years ago? This is just a ploy by the management to further cap our salaries. That's all.' People nod and someone else chips in, 'And we will also have to say goodbye to a few of our colleagues.' The derailment of the transformation had started.

As always, unaddressed anti-stories do not vanish. They just float across to the coffee-vending machines.

Having identified the anti-stories through story listening, we need to use the influence story structure discussed in Chapter 6 to address them. In the example above, the HR director used the same structure to address the concerns. He said, 'Some of you might be thinking that the new performance management system will cap salaries. I can see where you are coming from. Last time, the rapid salary growth slowed down exactly around the time the last performance system was introduced. That was just a coincidence. The two were not related. Two years ago, this system was introduced in two other countries—Germany and Thailand. In both the countries, it has worked very well. In fact, in both countries the employee engagement scores have gone up. That is why I believe this is going to work as well. I need all of you to support the change and get the same kind of results that Germany and Thailand got.'

This may not change the potential sceptics into raving fans, but it would surely ensure that cynicism didn't grow its roots.

So, here were a few ways in which story listening can be used. Wherever messy people issues are present, using stories to identify patterns is a very powerful approach.

Managing Change through Stories

A s I write this, Amazon.in throws up 28,775 search results for 'books on change management' in the business, strategy and management section alone. Change management is a collective term for all approaches to prepare and support individuals, teams and organizations in making organizational change.

This is clearly an area of struggle and concern for most leaders. I remember reading a Dilbert comic strip once where the pointy haired boss informs everyone in a meeting: 'We're hiring a director of change management to help employees embrace strategic changes.' To this, Dilbert says, 'Or we could come up with strategies that make sense. Then employees would embrace change.' The pointy haired boss replies, 'That sounds harder.'

Moving from comedy to reality, John Kotter, the guru of organizational change, published a paper in 1995 on the eight biggest errors that can doom a change exercise.[1] After studying over 100 companies that had attempted transformations, the eight major challenges he identified were: generating a sense of urgency, establishing a powerful guiding coalition, developing a vision, communicating the vision clearly, removing obstacles, planning for and creating short-term wins, avoiding premature declaration of victory and embedding change in the corporate culture.

My last five years of work with stories have proven that, in at least three of the eight challenges listed above, using stories or story structures can be enormously beneficial. They are: communicating the vision clearly, generating a sense of urgency and embedding change in the corporate culture.

Change is most acceptable when one understands both what the change is all about and the reason behind the change. It could be your corporate strategy, your culture transformation programme, your merger strategy or even one of your business line strategies—anything that involves major change.

Change is energized by:

1. An inspiring purpose, for which we use a clarity story and tackle anti-stories.
2. The leadership team's ability to engage, influence and inspire people, which is where storytelling skills come in.
3. A process to regularly share stories on how to do it right, where we use success stories.

All three parts are needed to succeed. The clarity story sets the direction and inspires action. Finding and acknowledging anti-stories quells the naysayers. Story skills provide the communication capability that helps leaders explain what needs to happen, and why it matters. Success stories are the fuel to keep the system fired up. Each new success provides evidence of progress and a huge dose of motivation. Let us understand this with an example.

> Imagine you are the head of the delivery centre of a global software service provider. You lead a team of over 50,000 people based in India. Your company has business development personnel based in the USA, who meet potential clients and source projects. You and your team work on designing and deploying solutions for clients. While this model of onshore business development and offshore solutions development has worked successfully over the last decade, things are now slowing down, and you want your team in India to identify new businesses and acquire them. This is a very big change as you are going to be asking engineers, more comfortable behind the computer screen, to actually sell. The task is clearly not as easy as telling your team that 'from this year one of our deliverables is to get new business. Our performance appraisal and our reward mechanism would be aligned to the same.' I am sure you can anticipate the bewilderment in your team and the pushback you will get.

Let us see how you can increase your chances of success by using the story approach discussed above: using a clarity story, addressing anti-stories, teaching leaders story skills and using success stories.

Creating the Clarity Story

This involves casting the change message into a clarity story structure, identifying anti-stories and addressing them. Here is what you finally share when you decide to kick off this initiative during the annual off-site:

Hi, today I am going to share an exciting addition to our job description that will initially feel challenging, and even daunting, but will definitely enrich the work that we do and help the company in a big way.

In the Past

It's been a great decade for our company. We have delivered strong growth over this period and, today, we are the number one choice for clients looking for software solutions. The team in India has played a very critical role in making that happen by ensuring that all the business that has been sourced by our colleagues in sales have been delivered on cost and on time, every time.

These ten years have seen us work on large projects for large clients. Our depth of knowledge and experiences in the technologies we use have been second to none.

Then Something Happened

But that easy journey to our annual targets seems to be becoming a thing of the past. You all know that as a company we met our targets last year, but only just, and that too with a lot of uncertainty till the very end. This happened as pressures on costs have put a squeeze on the IT budgets of our client companies. The project sizes the clients are sending request for proposals (RFPs) are much smaller. Hence, the number of new deals we need to win is much more for the same turnover.

The increase in the speed of introduction of new technologies has also thrown up a challenge. While we, at the delivery centre, have people who have invested in learning newer and newer technologies, the sales teams are still more comfortable with selling the older solutions. All this has resulted in the company finding it difficult to hit targets with the ease it is used to.

So Now

We now need to look at a different approach. Just asking our sales colleagues to get large projects from newer and newer clients is going to get increasingly difficult. We need to also find smaller projects with current clients, and that is where we all come in. The sales colleagues' relationship and interaction with the clients reduces dramatically once the project is awarded and the ongoing development starts. This is when this delivery team needs to be in constant engagement with the client. Since we are working alongside our client teams for our project, we are also privy to discussions about other challenges the client is facing. That puts us in a great position to spot additional opportunities in the client's businesses. We are also able to spot openings where new technologies can be used to increase effectiveness in areas the clients themselves may not have seen.

So, we have decided to add a new dimension to our work—that of generating new business. We will now all have a sales target along with our targets on cost and speed of delivery that we have always had. For this, we do not have to go out and meet new people and pitch for business. We will do it by upselling and cross-selling solutions to our clients. We will do it by identifying opportunities where new technologies can be deployed for increasing effectiveness and efficiency of client's systems. I know that with our understanding of their business and our relationships with them, we will be able to bring in new business for our company. This will help augment the business that will continue to be developed by our sales colleagues.

Tackling an Anti-Story

Some of you may be thinking: 'How on earth am I going to do selling? I am, after all, a technical person.' I understand that, but I also believe that our understanding of our client businesses, and our relationship with them, will make this more like finding better solutions for them than going on cold calls. Just last week, Ravi and his team actually closed a half-a-million-dollar deal. As you all know, for the last year or so, Ravi has been working on the front-end sales automation project with one of our large FMCG clients. During the project, Ravi and his team noticed that optimal use of the sales automation was not happening because the back-end systems, like sourcing and supply chain, were still running on legacy systems. During one of the review meetings, Ravi presented an option to the client where upgrading the back-end systems would not only increase efficiencies in the front-end sales system, but also lead to a huge cost reduction in the whole supply chain. After further discussions, the client awarded us the contract. This happened because Ravi and his team, who are embedded in the client's company, were able to spot the opportunity. And because of our proven delivery capabilities, the client did not hesitate to give us the contract. This is why I am certain that all of us will be able to do the same.

In the Future

As we go ahead and make this effort of new business generation successful, we will not only be able to augment our business development efforts and ensure that we meet and exceed our target, but we will achieve much more. We will be adding a new skill to our repertoire. We will be able to help clients make their systems even more effective and hence contribute phenomenally to their success. This will also ensure that our chances of remaining the partner of choice increase.

I look forward to soon hearing about the successes you and your team are having in spotting and converting new opportunities. All the very best!

This is how the change message could be crafted using the clarity story structure. Also, this is how anti-stories can be replaced with a more powerful story.

We discussed in Chapter 7 the three main reasons why change messaging doesn't stick: abstraction of language, absence of context, and 'the curse of knowledge'. Using the clarity story structure helps overcome all these.

Employees can only display new behaviours if they know what is expected of them and why. Hearing the change message in a story format achieves this.

Even though you are not from this imaginary company, if I asked you to put this book down and share the global software service providers' transformation message to someone, would you be able to do it? I am sure you would. When we are told the change message as a narrative, we are able to harness the three powers of stories: stories are easy to understand, stories are easy to remember and stories are easy to retell.

Teaching Story Skills

The clarity story that has been put together using the previous step is most powerfully delivered orally. Putting it into a PowerPoint deck obviously kills most of the impact. In order to share this orally we need to teach the leaders storytelling skills, the same skills that we have been discussing in this book. Many leaders will be apprehensive as this is not how they communicated before. However, as you have seen for yourself, it is neither rocket science nor unnatural. A little bit of training and some practice is all it takes.

The trick is to keep in mind the following premises. First, one should learn business storytelling from people from the business world, people who have worked extensively in organizations and understand the business context completely. Second, focus on making it a habit. This is done through deliberate practice. The third way is to find ways to be exposed to multiple examples of successful use of stories in business. It really is that simple.

Sharing Success Stories

To ensure that the change message really sticks, we need lots of stories from people that illustrate the new way or new behaviour in action. Creating a systematic process of finding and broadcasting positive stories across the organization is a powerful method to achieve this.

One way to approach this is to first choose a few themes from the change that have been proposed in the new strategy. The themes could be specific actions people need to take or specific behaviour the employees need to display for the change to be successful. In the example used above, the themes could be: spotting related opportunities for the projects they are already doing with clients, identifying opportunities to leverage new technologies, or successfully converting such opportunities into sale. The reason I would recommend all three and not just the third—successful sale—is that we must reward the behaviours we want the employees to display. Not all opportunities will be converted, but the behaviour of discovery needs to be encouraged.

Once the themes are identified, you can initially run anecdote circles to collect positive stories. As discussed earlier, not all stories will be a correct representation of the action or behaviour we are looking for and hence we need to select from among the collected stories the ones that correctly demonstrate the change we are looking for.

The next step is to get the leaders, who have been taught storytelling skills, to share these stories across the organization in both one-to-one and one-to-many situations.

This is where we can harness the power of the digital medium. Since oral storytelling is the most powerful way to share this message, videos of leaders telling these stories work almost as well as a live session. These videos can easily be shared across the organization using the intranet, Facebook and WhatsApp groups.

It is through listening to these stories that employees keep building a better understanding of what action and behaviour is expected of them. The sharing of stories has the added advantage of recognizing the people who live this change and creating peer pressure for others to follow. Finally, these stories also give the senior leadership an often required jolt of motivation to keep at it.

The final step in the success stories journey is to create a process through which employees can continue to get inspired and tell their own stories.

Every day, in every Apple retail store across the world, all the employees gather to talk about the Net Promoter Scores (NPS) collected the day before.[2] If someone gets a high NPS, the manager calls it out: 'Hey everyone, Jenny got a great NPS yesterday.' The staff members clap. The manager then wants everyone to know how this was achieved. 'Jenny, can you share with us what happened with that guy who came in with the iPad mini?'

So Jenny tells the story of the great service this customer received.

Because Apple's employees are regaled every day with stories of great customer service, they all know what it looks like. They are not forced to remember so-called inspirational posters with corny customer service acronyms. Instead, they get praise from their managers—and they get the chance to tell their colleagues the concrete details of what happened.

By using a story structure to share an inspiring purpose, and by sharing stories of the change being successful, we can increase our chances of managing the change successfully. With that we can hope to achieve what Dilbert had said: 'Come up with strategies that make sense. Then employees would embrace change.'

Storytelling for the Super Salesman

'**M**Y WALLPAPER AND I are fighting a duel to death—one or the other of us has to go,' joked Oscar Wilde as he lay dying in Hôtel d'Alsace in Paris's Rue des Beaux-Arts. On 30 November 1900, the wallpaper won the duel and Wilde, only forty-six at that time, succumbed to cerebral meningitis.

The wallpaper is still preserved in room number 16 of the hotel that is now called L'Hotel. The walls around the window are candy-striped. The others are lined with green and gold peacocks gently kissing each other.

The room also has many other Wilde memorabilia— his writing desk, a framed copy of his final bill at the hotel and a copy of the letter from the hotel manager asking Wilde—addressed as Sebastian Melmoth, as he called himself then—to pay the bill. Wilde was unable to as, he said in a letter to a friend, 'I am dying above my means.'

Today, tourists are happy to pay €700 a night for that room while similar rooms in the hotel cost around €500.

That is the power of the story.

The story behind objects dramatically changes the value of the same. If you were to visit my home, you would find an unremarkable collection of stones of different shapes, hues and textures on a table in one corner of the living room. But when my wife explains the origins of each of the stones— glaciers in Alaska, mountain streams in the Himalayas, ancient forests, high-altitude deserts—the stones take on a different image. They transform from being merely stones to precious moments frozen in time.

Eight miles from Edinburgh in Scotland is a small hamlet called Roslin. The chapel in Roslin catapulted into limelight in 2006. Dan Brown fans will recognize this as the Rosslyn Chapel from the bestseller *The Da Vinci Code*.[1] The book, about the existence of a bloodline of Jesus, was made into a movie in 2006 starring Tom Hanks and Audrey Tautou. While there is no mystical rose line running through the chapel, no Star of David carved on the floor or a hidden vault where the fabled Holy Grail may rest—all claims made in the book, it has not stopped tourists from thronging to Roslin. The crowd had swelled from the usual 30,000-odd a year to 1,20,000 after the release of the novel in 2003. The movie took it up to 1,80,000 in 2006.

In fact, Scotland's tourism agency, Visit Scotland, joined forces with Sony Pictures—the producers of the movie—to encourage tourists to visit the locations used in the movie. This promotion was run in forty countries across the world. Scottish Tourism estimates they received more than £6 million worth of free publicity as a result. Not a bad number!

Dan Brown's books have seen tourist numbers swell in Paris (*The Da Vinci Code*), Rome and Washington DC (*The Lost Symbol*) and Florence (*Inferno*). That again is the power of a story.

This power is not unknown to successful people involved in sales around the world. As a senior sales manager of one of the world's largest B2B companies told me, 'The top 20 per cent of my team outsell the others by a large margin. All of them are natural storytellers. Imagine what we could do if we helped the next 20–30 per cent learn this skill.' This difference in the sales numbers is in line with the findings from a study conducted among over 6000 salespeople in more than ninety companies by research firm CEB, which showed that the gap between average-performing salespeople and star performers is close to 200 per cent for solution sales.

This means the 'helping the next 30 per cent learn the skill of storytelling' can bump up sales of the entire team by 20 per cent. There is clearly a very valuable opportunity here for companies to help their average performers improve and close the gap.

While the impact of using stories during the sales process is very high across sectors and industries, the biggest impact is in B2B companies where the frontline's conversation with the client is the only method of persuasion. Unlike B2C companies, these teams don't have the luxury of a high-decibel advertising campaign backing their sales efforts.

Let us now see how the various story patterns we learnt in Part II of the book can be used during the sales process.

Regardless of the specific steps you follow, there are four things you need to do to help customers get what they need.

First, you need to build a rapport with your customer. People buy *you* first. People don't care about your ideas unless they care about you. Stories about you and your company, as we will discuss later in the chapter, are a great way to do this.

Second, you need to establish your credibility. It's clear that in B2B sales, corporate credibility is important, but so is personal credibility. The prospective client needs to know whether you and the company deliver what you promise. Are you reliable? Do you understand your client's needs? Are you responsive to those needs? Stories are at the heart of building such credibility.

Third, you need to demonstrate value. The acclaimed management consultant Tom Peters had said that the secret of business success was to make the consumer 'delighted' with the product or service. The information you share at the pitch, the oral or in the proposal, should be able to show the consumer how you really understand their business and why your product or service will give them more than what they came looking for. The story you tell will be most effective when you develop it with your customer, so that when they receive your proposal it's familiar—as much their story as yours.

Finally, you need to close the deal. Here again we need to master the skill of handling objections. We know that our standard approach to counter arguments with data is often unsuccessful. This is because you can never replace a story with a fact. You need to replace it with another powerful story.

Now let's look at each of the four steps in detail.

Building Rapport

In order to build a rapport with our customers we can use two different story structures: connection story and success story.

Connection story is a story pattern we covered in Chapter 5. Through anecdotes, when you talk about yourself, one of two things is achieved. You may establish that you are like your customer—similar values, similar beliefs or similar backgrounds. Famed influence psychologist Robert Caildini has shown that we are most influenced by people like us. This is achieved not by telling your customer that you are just like them. Rather, let them work that out by telling them a story that illustrates this.

The second part of building a rapport is getting the customer to come to the conclusion that he or she is dealing with a team and company that has been successful in helping clients like him or her. Again, a claim will not do. Use a success story. As discussed in Chapter 8, success stories are case studies but they are not written in the usual cold, dry, formulaic manner—full of jargon, claims and assertions, often trying to oversell. Instead, they are written in a way that the customer can resonate with the client in the case study, understand that he or she feels the same way, and be able to anticipate that he or she, too, can enjoy the same success if he or she decides to use your product or service. Narrating your successful case studies in this manner harnesses the three big powers of stories we have been talking about in this book— stories are easy to understand, stories are easy to remember and stories are easy to retell. This way, the knowledge of your success remains with your customer.

Establishing Credibility

This phase is about building trust. We know that people first buy us before they buy our products or services. So the prospective client needs to know whether they can trust you and your company to deliver what you promise you would. It is also very important to demonstrate your knowledge of a customer's business and its economic drivers. Stories are at the heart of building this credibility.

You can share a success story about something that happened in a business similar to theirs, and how it was tackled. If it is unexpected and better than what they have currently, you have just provided an insight.

All successful companies are always sitting on a gold mine of great examples of how they have made a significant difference to their clients' life and business. However, at best those are available as boring case studies. All it requires is a little effort to convert them into a short oral success story as discussed in Chapter 8. A little story like this is an analogy for many types of business problems and helps the customer think differently.

Demonstrating Value

Your proposal should tell the story of why the suggested action is needed and how it will address the needs of the business. A very effective structure for this is the clarity story structure discussed in Chapter 7. The narrative usually begins with how things were in the past, which your solution would impact. But then something changed, there were some turning points that necessitated our doing something different now—your solution. You then get into describing that solution. Finally, the narrative ends by painting a picture of the future, of what success will look like to people within the buyers' organization.

The story you tell will be most effective when you develop it with your customer. You ask them how they were handling the situation in the past and why that approach was working. This gives you the material for the first part of the clarity story—*In the past*. You then ask them what challenges they are facing now. You then introduce the changes in technology and approach that have happened and can help them solve those challenges. These two things that are forcing us to change and things that will enable us to change give us the second part— *Then something happened*. Now you introduce the solution you are proposing, your product or service that will solve the problem. This gives you the third part—*So Now*. Finally you discuss what life would be like after the solution is adopted and what could be the further steps. This makes up the fourth part of the clarity story—*In the future*. When you co-create the clarity story with your client, it becomes as much his story as yours. He can then use it when he tries to sell your solution internally to his or her team and other decision makers.

Asking For The Business

This is where, like in any other sales process, we need to be adept at handling objections. Objections are nothing but stories people have in their head about why what they believe in is true. As discussed earlier, it is virtually impossible to fight a story with a fact. Not only is providing evidence to discredit a belief ineffective, it can also work against the objective by triggering the confirmation bias. Research conducted by Lord, Ross and Lepper (1979)[2] suggests that people will not only persevere in their original beliefs but may come to believe in them even more strongly. It is only possible to dislodge such beliefs by replacing them with another story. This is where we use the influence story pattern discussed in Chapter 6, where instead of pushing people to change their mind using data, we narrate incidences and anecdotes which demonstrate the existence of an alternative reality, a new possibility, and let the listener pull this in and replace the current story in their mind.

So, go ahead and teach your sales team to use connection stories, success stories, clarity stories and influence stories, and see the average salesperson turn into a super one. Remember, even if only the second 20 per cent performs like the first, it will dramatically increase overall sales.

Presentation and Storytelling

ABOUT THREE WEEKS ago, I was in Las Vegas to speak at a conference. I was staying at the Four Seasons hotel. The barista there was amazing. He made great coffee, knew many of the patrons by name and was really engaging. People would line up for a second coffee just to talk with him. His name was Noah. I spoke to him about his exceptional customer service.

He explained that he loved making great coffee and interacting with customers. 'I guess I'm just a people person,' Noah explained. I asked him what it was like working at the Four Seasons, and he told me how great it was and how he could be himself. 'Managers here look after me. When I'm busy, they ask if they can help froth the milk or do anything else. If I ask for anything,' he explained, 'they make it happen.'

It turns out that Noah has a young family and that being a barista doesn't pay that well. To make ends meet, he has a second job as a barista at Caesars Palace. 'What's it like working there, do you get the same response from customers there?' I asked. Noah explained 'It's completely different there. If the managers there notice you, it's because you've done something wrong. I just keep my head down, make great coffee and avoid talking to customers.'

With this story, Simon Sinek started his keynote address at Association for Talent Development (ATD) 2016 as 10,000-odd participants leant in to listen. Simon was wearing a pair of jeans and a long-sleeved shirt. He didn't have a PowerPoint presentation but just used a flip chart and markers.

After sharing the story, Simon turned to the flip chart and drew a circle. Inside the circle, he wrote 'safety', and outside the circle he wrote 'fear'. He turned back to the audience and asked, 'What environment are your managers creating? If your staff feel safe, chances are they'll be giving great customer service. If they feel fear, chances are your company is providing substandard customer service and your customers are probably going somewhere else.'

That evening, during the international networking event, as Mark Schenk from Anecdote mingled among the crowd, he asked what they remembered most from the day. Almost all of them mentioned Simon Sinek's talk. They remembered Noah the barista, they remembered the story about different supervisory experiences he was having, and most of them would draw an imaginary circle and talk about the difference between safety and fear. They didn't just remember the story but also the message Simon wanted to convey.

Mark then asked the same people what they remembered from the talk given by the speaker before Simon Sinek. Not a single person could recall that. Some even said, 'Was there a speaker before Simon?' Only one person remembered a part of the content, but he asked, 'Didn't he mention how Kodak went out of business?' However, he couldn't remember the point the speaker was making.

In his blog piece about this incidence, Mark goes on to describe the speaker before Simon Sinek. He writes:

> You might be thinking that this guy was a poor presenter. On the contrary, he was an excellent presenter. He strode on to the stage wearing a Versace suit, Italian leather shoes and a Madonna-style microphone. He was tall, slim and handsome, and commanded the stage like the seasoned professional he was. He moved around the stage without notes, delivered a word-perfect presentation with a multimedia mega show, music, videos, interviews—it was a presentation coach's wet dream.

The problem was that the speaker was focussed on giving an impressive presentation and making statements like, 'SAP has standardized and simplified its content governance procedures . . .' Mark writes that he immediately jotted this down because he knew he would forget it within seconds if he didn't.

That is the difference between speaking to share and speaking to shine. If you would like your audience to understand, remember and even retell your message hours after you finish your presentation, then using stories and story structures is perhaps the only way.

Now, let's talk about using stories, story structures and story patterns in our presentations. But before I get into how we can do so, I want to talk about the beginning and the end. I will share the three worst ways to start a presentation or a speech, the three best ways to start and the three best ways to end.

Three Worst Ways to Start a Speech

The third worst way to start a speech is by thanking the people who invited you and expressing gratitude for the opportunity to speak in front of the august crowd. What is wrong about being grateful? Nothing. Just don't do it at the start. Research has shown that we form opinions about a person in the first seven seconds of his appearance based on what we see and the non-verbal cues we get. We make up our minds in the first twenty-one seconds of the person speaking whether we would like to listen to them or not. So, the first twenty-eight seconds are the most valuable to reel in attention and the desire to listen. Why would you waste that in an acknowledgement of indebtedness? I am not saying that you can't verbalize gratefulness, just don't do it at the start.

The second worst way is to clear your throat. The funny sound of an old Lambretta scooter trying to start reverberates from the speaker. Not a pleasant sound. You then slap the cordless mic on your chest and ask 'Is this working? Can you guys hear me at the back?' Then you look at the screen and move a few slides back and forth to check if the remote is working. All these tell the audience, loud and clear, that you don't respect them or their time. If you did, you would have come an hour early and done the equipment check and warmed up your vocal chords.

The absolutely worst way to start a speech is by introducing yourself and the topic you will speak on. For instance, 'Good morning, my name is Indranil Chakraborty and I am the founder of StoryWorks. Today, I am going to talk to you about the power of business storytelling.'

Since over 90 per cent of the speakers I have heard start their speeches this way, why is it the worst? Well, the speaker's name and topic has been hammered at you several times already. You read it in the invite, your calendar reminder probably mentioned it, the agenda in front of you has that information, and in all likelihood it is the cover slide of the presentation which is already up on the screen.

This beginning is a clear signal to the audience that this is a good time to take out their smartphones, reconnect with office and check if their absence was missed, and whether there are any crises that need to be attended to before moving on to Facebook.

Three Best Ways to Start a Speech

The third best way to start a speech is by using an 'imagine' scenario. 'Imagine a big explosion as you climb up 3000 ft.

Imagine a plane full of smoke. Imagine an engine going clack, clack, clack. It sounds scary. Well, I had a unique seat that day. I was sitting on 1D.' This is how Ric Elias started his TED talk—'3 Things I Learned While My Plane Crashed'[1]— on the Hudson river landing. This true story was captured in an award-winning film, *Sully*, starring Tom Hanks.

The second is to start with a statistic or factoid that shocks. Jamie Oliver, a British celebrity chef, restauranteur and activist who promotes healthy eating among children, started his TED Talk—'Teach Every Child about Food'[2]—with 'Sadly, in the next eighteen minutes when I do our chat, four Americans that are alive will be dead through the food that they eat.' Given that the audience here was mainly American, there is no way that it didn't get their attention.

The absolutely best way to start a speech—no points for guessing—is with a story, one that is inextricably linked with the topic you are speaking on. 'I was only four years old when I saw my mother load a washing machine for the very first time in her life. That was a great day for her. My mother and father had been saving money for years to be able to buy that machine, and the first day it was going to be used, even Grandma was invited to see the machine. And Grandma was even more excited. Throughout her life she had been heating water with firewood, and she had hand-washed laundry for seven children. And now she was going to watch electricity do that work.' This is how one of my favourite TED speakers, Hans Rosling, a physician, academic, statistician, and public speaker started his TED Talk—'The Magic Washing Machine'[3]—about the greatest invention of the Industrial Revolution. As we have been discussing throughout this book, stories draw in the listeners and makes them lean forward. What would be a better way to start!

Three Best Ways to Finish a Speech

The third best way to finish is with a call to action. After all, the reason we deliver a speech or give a presentation is that we want to change the status quo. We want people to act on the information we give them because they now think differently about the topic based on your speech or presentation. Amy Cuddy, a Harvard professor and author of the book *Presence*,[4] is also the speaker of the second-most viewed TED Talk ever—'Your Body Language May Shape Who You Are'.[5] In her talk, she argues that 'power posing'—standing in a posture of confidence even when we don't feel confident—can boost feelings of confidence and might have an impact on our chances for success. She finishes her speech with a call to action—'So I want to ask you first, you know, both to try power posing, and also I want to ask you to share the science, because this is simple. I don't have ego involved in this. Give it away. Share it with people, because the people who can use it the most are the ones with no resources and no technology and no status and no power. Give it to them because they can do it in private. They need their bodies, privacy and two minutes, and it can significantly change the outcomes of their lives.'

The second best way is to end with a rhetorical question. Based on your talk or presentation, the answer to this question is fairly obvious, but you let the audience answer it in their heads. They leave the presentation with the question and their answers lingering in their minds.

One of the most famous rhetorical questions in political history came during a 1980 presidential debate between challenger Ronald Reagan, and the incumbent, President Jimmy Carter. Governor Reagan scored a knockout blow by finishing the debate with a series of rhetorical questions, the first of which became his most famous:

> Next Tuesday is Election Day. Next Tuesday, all of you will go to the polls, will stand there in the polling place and make a decision. I think when you make that decision, it might be well if you would ask yourself, are you better off than you were four years ago? Is it easier for you to go and buy things in the stores than it was four years ago? Is there more or less unemployment in the country than there was four years ago? Is America as respected throughout the world as it was? Do you feel that our security is as safe, that we're as strong as we were four years ago? And if your answer to all of those questions is yes, why then, I think your choice is very obvious as to whom you will vote for. If you don't agree, if you don't think that this course that we've been on for the last four years is what you would like to see us follow for the next four, then I could suggest another choice that you have.

The best way to end, however, is with a story. If it can be related to the story you began with, there is nothing better than that. Like the end of Hans Rosling's speech which started with the washing machine—'My mother explained the magic with this machine the very, very first day. She said, "Now, Hans, we have loaded the laundry. The machine will make the work.

And now we can go to the library." Because this is the magic: you load the laundry, and what do you get out of the machine? You get books out of the machines, children's books. And Mother got time to read for me. She loved this. I got the "ABCs"—this is where I started my career as a professor, when my mother had time to read for me. And she also got books for herself. She managed to study English and learn that as a foreign language. And she read so many novels, so many different novels here. And we really, really loved this machine.'

Having covered the best ways to start and end a presentation—with a story—let's discuss how else we can use the stories and story structures this book talks about.

We have spoken earlier about the fact that your listeners need to first buy you first before they buy your idea, product or service. And what they buy about you is character. If the presentation is to a person you have never met before, or an audience who doesn't really know you, a connection story is an important element to keep handy. When should you use it? Sometimes, you can use it at the beginning if the format requires you to start with an introduction. And if your connection story is also linked with the topic of the presentation, that is truly a bonanza.

Brené Brown, a research professor at the University of Houston, started her very popular TED Talk—'The Power of Vulnerability'—[6] with this story.

> So, I'll start with this: a couple of years ago, an event planner called me because I was going to do a speaking event. And she called, and she said, 'I'm really struggling with how to write about you on the little flyer.' And I thought, 'Well,

what's the struggle? And she said, 'Well, I saw you speak, and I'm going to call you a researcher, I think, but I'm afraid that if I call you a researcher, no one will come, because they'll think you're boring and irrelevant.'

And I was like, 'Okay.' And she said, 'But the thing I liked about your talk is that you're a storyteller. So I think what I'll do is just call you a storyteller.' And of course, the academic, insecure part of me was like, 'You're going to call me a what?' And she said, 'I'm going to call you a storyteller.' And I was like, 'Why not "magic pixie"?'

I continued, 'Let me think about this for a second.' I tried to call deep on my courage. And I thought, you know, I am a storyteller. I'm a qualitative researcher. I collect stories; that's what I do. And maybe stories are just data with a soul. And maybe I'm just a storyteller. And so I said, 'You know what? Why don't you just say I'm a researcher–storyteller.'

The story took less than a minute to tell, but it does speak to us about Brené. It exposes her vulnerability—'the academic, insecure part of me'—endears her to the audience and fits in well with the subject of her talk.

The other option is to weave it in as part of the presentation. Imagine that I have been asked to speak on the power of story work for a marketer. During the presentation, in the section about insights, I start with Gary Klein's quote: 'Insight is when you unexpectedly come to a better story.' I then tell this story.

In 1998, I was appointed as the brand manager for Lifebuoy in India. Lifebuoy was still a carbolic brick-shaped soap which hadn't changed much since its inception in 1933.

Even though it was still the highest-selling soap in the world, it was largely used by people in the lower income group and in rural India. In order to understand the consumer better, I decided to spend a few days in a village. One of the beliefs we all had was that people bought Lifebuoy because of its promise of health. After all, the jingle, '*Tandoroosti ki raksha karta hai* Lifebuoy, Lifebuoy *hain jahan, tandoroosti hai wahan*' (Lifebuoy protects your health. Lifebuoy ensures a healthy life) was something every Indian could sing even if he or she didn't use the brand. However, the consumer survey scores on the attribute 'I use Lifebuoy because it protects my health' were actually lower than 'I use Lifebuoy because it gives me value for my money.'

During my stay in the village, I met an old man who had never bathed with soaps. I asked him why and he replied, 'Why should I?' I said that his work as a farmer would literally get his hands dirty and that dirt contains germs and germs could cause ill health. Hence, by bathing with Lifebuoy he could remain healthy. He laughed his head off and said, '*Beta, agar* Lifebuoy *se tandoroost hota toh main usey kat kat ke kha leta!*' (Son, if Lifebuoy meant good health, I would cut it into pieces and eat it). It was at that moment that I realized that while people knew the jingle, the connection between Lifebuoy and health was not clear to many people. This insight, my unexpected discovery of a better story, caused me to ensure that going forward, I would explain the laddering explicitly in our brand communication. The line used in Lifebuoy ads decades ago was brought back. It went like, 'Lifebuoy *mael mein chhupe kitanuo ko dho dalta hai, roam roam tak karta tandoroosti ki raksha'* (Lifebuoy washes away germs hidden in dirt from every pore and protects your health). This new communication increased the consumer scores on 'I use Lifebuoy because it protects my health.'

While I tell this anecdote to illustrate how story listening can help garner insight, it also tells a lot about me. It lets the audience come to various conclusions which increases my credibility as a speaker on the subject of marketing—I did successfully handle one of the most iconic brands in India. I am hard-working and happy to get my hands dirty. I am passionate about what I do. I am able to connect the dots, etc. All these, you will agree, would go a long way in connecting with the audience of marketers.

That was the use of a connection story.

Probably the most useful story structure to use is the clarity story structure. The first two sections of 'in the past' and 'then something happened' do a great job of setting up the context. As discussed in Chapter 7, you don't spend too much time on this, but it is important to get people on the same page. The heart of the presentation is the next section. So now, here is where you talk about what you are proposing—the how, the when, etc. The last section of 'in the future' wraps up by talking about what the future would look like as a result of the actions, and also what the other positive, perhaps unintended, consequences of the action may be.

In the 'so now' section, you can also handle the anti-stories you anticipate by replacing them with a better story using the influence story structure. You must also keep stories ready to counter other objections or anti-stories you may hear. These are for the anti-stories that might come up, but you don't want to proactively address them as you are not sure if they are widely held beliefs.

Of course, sharing success stories in the right section of the presentation adds to your credibility and can be used to reassure the audience that you and your team are capable of delivering what you are talking about.

So, these are the various ways the story structure you learnt about in the book can make your presentations more impactful, easier to understand and memorable.

It would make sense at this point to address something that often confuses me. People often ask me, 'I am not sure my presentation is telling a good story. Can you help me?' This plea has increased over the years and often comes from people with a technical background working on pitches. I assume someone must have told them that their presentations need to have a story.

So, why does that confuse me? While a story, like a presentation, has a beginning, middle and an end, there is much more to it than just that. Like we discussed in Chapter 3, a story needs to have a time or location marker, a causal sequence of events, characters and a surprise ending. It is unlikely that all business presentations will necessarily have all those elements. That is why it doesn't make sense to talk about whether 'my presentation is telling a good story'. You might say that this is hair-splitting, but I think that while a presenter may tell a story—should tell a story—a presentation doesn't always have to.

What the presentation must have is a story structure.

Let me reiterate the difference between a story and a story structure. There are various story structures that I will describe below. The oft-quoted basic would be a beginning, middle and an end. But you might rightly say that the same holds true for a sewage pipe.

Here are a few robust plot structures you can use. The first is Freytag's pyramid, which is also referred to as the mountain. It goes like this:

1. **Exposition:** Background information of the plot that includes character and setting.
2. **Initial incident:** The first conflict that occurs in the plot.
3. **Rising action:** Events that add suspense or tension to the plot (complications or frustrations), which leads to the climax.
4. **Climax:** The most suspenseful part of the plot, also often the turning point for the protagonist.
5. **Falling action:** Events that unravel the conflict between the protagonist and the antagonist, which leads to the resolution.
6. **Resolution:** The conflict is resolved and we discover whether the protagonist achieves his or her goal or not.
7. **Denouement:** The 'tying up of loose ends'.

It is a good structure to describe a hurdle that your project, brand or company faced. Then share the various things that were tried but did not work—this shows that progress was not easy. Finally, describe the approach that worked and then the way forward.

The second is the monomyth, or the famous hero's journey, as first described by Joseph Campbell in his 1949 book, *The Hero with a Thousand Faces*.[7] This structure leverages the metaphor of a journey and can be used very powerfully when describing the evolution of a brand or business. The basic idea is that a normal person living in an ordinary world gets a call to go on an epic adventure. He refuses initially but then meets a mentor. There are trials the person faces—ups and downs, gains and losses. But eventually, with the help of the mentor, he gains enough skills to achieve his goal. He then returns to his original, normal life which will never be the same again as he now has new understanding and skills which he can share with others. For a more detailed version of the monomyth, you could read the very popular screenwriting textbook by Christopher Vogler, *The Writer's Journey: Mythic Structures for Writers*.[8]

The third is 'Sparklines', a concept written by Nancy Duarte in her book *Resonate: Present Visual Stories that Transform Audiences*.[9] This structure is a series of movements between what is and what could be. The structure helps you see contrasts. Duarte uses two speeches to demonstrate the power of this structure. Jawaharlal Nehru's 'Tryst with Destiny' and Martin Luther King's 'I Have a Dream' are speeches where the speakers start with what is and move back and forth between what is and what will be in an almost perfect frequency. They both end on a high, describing the new bliss, and with a call to action. This is a good structure to describe the various legs of a brand or business strategy.

The fourth is a favourite of mine. It is called 'in media res', which is Latin for 'into the middle of things'. Here, the presentation opens in the middle of the story's conflict, which is a great way to grab the audiences' attention by opening at the most interesting part of the presentation. This is also very useful when presenting to people who seem to be in a perpetual hurry and keep using phrases like 'cut to the chase'. A great example of this is a TED talk[10] which started like this:

> On 5 November 1990, a man named El-Sayyid Nosair walked into a hotel in Manhattan and assassinated Rabbi Meir Kahane, the leader of the Jewish Defense League. Nosair was initially found not guilty of the murder, but while serving time on lesser charges, he and other men began planning attacks on a dozen New York City landmarks, including tunnels, synagogues and the United Nations headquarters. Thankfully, those plans were foiled by an FBI informant. Sadly, the 1993 bombing of the World Trade Center was not. Nosair would eventually be convicted for his involvement in the plot. El-Sayyid Nosair is my father.

The speaker is Zak Ebrahim, and the title of the speech was 'I Am the Son of a Terrorist, Here's How I Chose Peace'. During the rest of his speech, Ebrahim recounts his childhood and the path he took after his father's conviction.

The fifth is the false start. This is when you begin to tell a seemingly predictable story before bringing in an unexpected twist and starting all over again. It is a great way to question usual patterns and beliefs and then talk about an innovation of dramatic change in approach, which leads to an unexpected or even better conclusion.

These are by no stretch of imagination an exhaustive list of structures but will hopefully give you enough thoughts about harnessing the power of stories in a presentation. A great way to add to these story structures is to listen to powerful TED talks and see whether they follow any of the above structures, or if you can discover another structure that you could use.

Coming back to stories, in addition to the overall story structure of the presentation, it would be great to use stories within the presentations to build context into numbers, highlight a point and turn abstract ideas concrete.

So, go ahead, use story structures in your presentations and tell individual stories with it, and see how you quickly get the tag of 'the best presenter' in your company.

Storytelling with Data

IN APRIL 2014, Ben Wellington, a professor of statistics
in New York, discovered something that initially did
not seem to make sense. Ben was playing around with
parking-ticket data, which had been made public by the
New York City government. In 2011, Mayor Bloomberg
had passed a legislation, called the open data law, which gave
regular citizens access to government data. This was what
allowed Ben to analyse the parking-ticket data. Ben focused
on the fines levied by the New York Police Department
(NYPD) for parking in front of fire hydrants. During the
analysis, Ben found that two hydrants on a particular street
in Manhattan had an absurdly high rate of getting cars
ticketed. Intrigued, he identified the fire hydrants on Google
Street View, and what he saw was surprising. The parking
spaces in front of both the hydrants were labelled 'parking
zones'. There was also a bike lane running next to the

parking space, and the fire hydrant was on the other side of the bike lane. Clearly the label of a valid parking zone and the distance from the fire hydrant made people feel that it was safe to park there. A bit of probing led to the discovery that while the Department of Transportation (DoT) marked it as a parking zone, the NYPD disagreed, causing the regular ticketing.

Ben published the analysis on his blog.[1] It caught the attention of publications like the *New York Observer*, the *New York Post* and the *Daily Mail*. All of them reached out to the DoT for comments. The initial response was that 'while DoT has not received any complaints about this location, we will review the roadway markings and make any appropriate alterations.' The DoT acted quickly, and by early June, both the spots were repainted as no-parking zones. Ben had saved the citizens of NYC $55,000 a year.

This data was always available with the government, but it was only when Ben told the story with the data that action was taken.

Another example is that of a man who could have saved many more lives if only he had told the story well.

In 1846, a Hungarian doctor, Ignaz Semmelweis,[2] was appointed as an assistant at a hospital in Vienna. The hospital had two maternity clinics to train doctors and midwives. At that time, many of the admitted mothers were dying of a mysterious illness called puerperal fever or childbed fever. The prevalent belief was that this was caused by 'miasma' or poisonous air. Very soon after joining,

Semmelweis noticed that in the wards staffed by doctors and medical students, the death rate was significantly more than the ones staffed by midwives.

Semmelweis collected the data over a few months. When he crunched the data, he saw that the mortality rate in the doctor's clinic was 9.9 per cent and in the midwives' clinic was 3.9 per cent. He refused to buy the poisonous gas theory and started looking out for differences between the doctors' and the midwives' wards, and tried to correct each one of them. When one action didn't work, he junked that idea and tried the next. Nothing worked.

His 'aha' moment was triggered by the unfortunate death of his friend Jakob Kolletschka. Kolletschka was a pathologist and had accidentally cut himself during an autopsy on one of the mothers who had died. When Semmelweis performed the post-mortem examination of his friend, he noticed a strong similarity in the pathology of his friend's illness and that of the women who died of childbed fever. This gave him a clue.

Semmelweis knew that many doctors performed autopsies in the morning and spent the rest of their day attending to patients in the maternity ward. The midwives, on the other hand, never came in contact with the corpse.

The concept of germs had not been established then. Louis Pasteur's discovery came twenty years later. So, Semmelweis conjectured that some kind of cadaver particles were being carried by the doctors into the maternity ward. He introduced a hand-wash process. The medical staff were ordered to clean their hands with a lime chlorine solution, which Semmelweis believed would wash away the poisonous particles. It worked!

The mortality rate, which was 12.2 per cent the previous month, fell to 2.2 per cent. After several months of lower mortality rate, he noticed that many medical students were still not adhering to the process. He introduced stricter controls and the mortality rates fell further. There were two months where there were no deaths due to childbed fever.

However, instead of celebrating his discovery and adopting his methods, the medical community ridiculed him. His theory went against their long-held belief about death being caused by poisonous gas. Semmelweis felt a deep frustration trying to convince doctors with his idea and was actually removed from his job a few months later. Sure enough, the hand-wash practice stopped and the mortality rates started climbing again.

Semmelweis had the data but was unable to tell a compelling story.

Perhaps the adoption would have been far higher had he been able to both contextualize the data and share a narrative. The Oxford English Dictionary defines a narrative as 'an account of a series of events, facts, etc., given in order and with the establishment of a connection between them'. Basically, a chain of causally related events.

In hindsight, he could have made the data personal by narrating individual stories of grief the families went through when a woman died during childbirth. He could have then gone on to visualize the data as shown in the diagram below and shared the narrative.

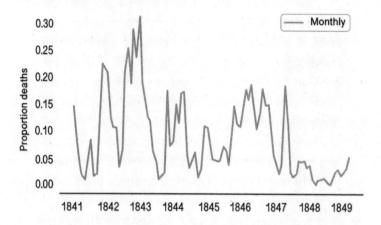

Data visualization is not the same as data storytelling. It aids the process of data storytelling. After all, a picture tells a thousand words.

A person who used data visualization and told a story to change people's mind about miasma, or poisonous air as a cause of death, was a doctor working in London at around the same time as Semmelweis.

John Snow was a doctor during the 1850s. Cholera came to London in 1832, and every four or five years, an outbreak would take between 10,000 and 20,000 lives. Here again, the dominant theory was that miasma was causing the death. There was indeed a stench hanging over London those days. Sewage infrastructure was still a thing of the future and most houses had a cesspool of human waste in their basement.

However, Snow believed that it wasn't the poisonous air but some kind of waterborne disease. He published a paper in 1849 called 'On the Mode of Communication of Cholera', but no one listened to him. The public health authorities largely ignored what he had to say. He had made the case in a number of papers and done a number of studies, but nothing had really stuck.

Then on 28 August 1854, a five-year-old girl, referred to as Baby Lewis in subsequent documents, somehow contracted cholera at 40 Broad Street in Soho. The outbreak that followed was deadly. Literally 10 per cent of the neighbourhood died in seven days. The casualty figure would have been much higher had the people in the surrounding area not fled after the initial outbreak. Snow lived nearby and was convinced that such a concentrated outbreak pointed to a single-point source. In the now famous map reproduced on the next page, Snow, working with a local priest—Reverend Henry Whitehead—plotted the location of deaths and the location of hand pumps used to draw water in the area. Deaths were marked by dashes and the pumps with a cross. When he looked at the annotated map, he observed that cholera occurred almost entirely among those who lived near and drank water from the Broad Street pump.

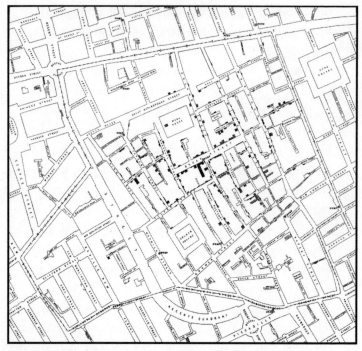

By John Snow [Public domain], via Wikimedia Commons

The irony was that this was a preferred pump in the neighbourhood. In his subsequent research paper, Snow wrote: 'There were only ten deaths in houses situated decidedly nearer to another street-pump. In five of these cases, the families of the deceased persons informed him that they always went to the pump on Broad Street, as they preferred its water to that of the pumps which were nearer. In three other cases, the deceased were children who went to school near the pump on Broad Street . . .' He then had the handle of the contaminated pump removed, ending the neighbourhood epidemic. Though the authorities promptly reinstalled the handle as soon as the outbreak died down, due to Snow's map and both his and Whitehead's continuous evangelizing, the authorities started coming around. By 1866, when the next big cholera outbreak happened in London, the authorities had been convinced by the story and the map that the water was a problem.[3]

Through storytelling and data visualization, Snow achieved what Semmelweis couldn't.

'Storytelling with data' is a nice catchphrase for impactful presentations which are data and analysis heavy. Storytelling presents two distinct and different uses.

One is the story structure of the entire presentation—we can use any one of the story structures discussed in the previous chapter (clarity story, Freytag's pyramid, monolith, sparklines, etc). The second comprises the stories individual data sets can tell. We need to ferret out these stories from the data and, in doing that, visualizing the data set is often a great aid.

Now, let's delve into the various analytic approaches we can use to discover stories we can tell with the data sets we have. Tableau Software is a US-based company which produces interactive data visualization products. The folks there have looked at the various kinds of analyses that people do on their data sets. They have concluded that there are at least seven approaches that can help us identify stories: change over time, contrast, intersection, outliers, factors, drill down and zoom in/out. They call them story types, but I disagree. Each approach and the subsequent visualization will help us identify stories but the analysis is not a story by itself.

Let's look at a few examples.

Change Over Time

This is when you have a time series data and there is an unanticipated change in the trajectory, and you tell the story about it.

Here is an example. In an article published in the *Wall Street Journal* titled 'Battling Infectious Diseases in the 20th Century: The Importance of Vaccines', the authors produced the heat map given below.

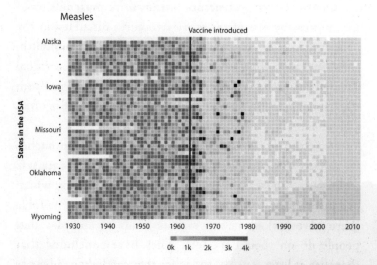

While the chart is a great example of data visualization, it doesn't tell the full story. Following the introduction of the measles vaccine in 1963, there was an immediate and dramatic reduction of incidences. The fact that the disease was almost eradicated in five years is not a story. It is still just information. This can trigger an inquiry into how people suffered with measles prior to the vaccine, what were the remedies they tried, how did the scientists come up with the vaccines, what were the various implementation challenges and how were they overcome. All these probes can help us tell the story.

The story below is made up of information from various sources on the Internet to give you an understanding of the story the data would help you tell.

> Measles is a disease that has tormented humans from time immemorial. The first written account was published by a Persian doctor in the ninth century. In the early 1900s, nearly all children got measles by the time they were fifteen years old. Some of them needed hospitalization, and a small percentage even succumbed to the disease. In the early 1950s, John F. Enders and Dr Thomas C. Peebles were trying to isolate the measles virus in the blood and create a vaccine. They succeeded in 1954 when several students contracted the disease in Boston, Massachusetts, during a measles outbreak. In 1963, Enders created a vaccine and licensed it in the USA. The Centre for Disease Control (CDC) ensured a widespread distribution and inoculation across the United States of America. Within the next five years, measles was virtually eradicated.

Now this is a story. Let's look at the story elements used here that we have earlier discussed in the book.

1. **Time/location Markers:** 1954 to 1964, Boston and then the whole of the USA.

2. **Sequence of Events:** isolating the measles virus, creating and licensing the vaccine, CDC implementation of widespread inoculation, eradication of measles.

3. **The 'aha' Moment:** vaccines eradicate measles in five years—an ancient disease that has plagued humankind for centuries.

The analytical approach—spotting a dramatic change in a time series data allowed us to probe and discover a story behind the change. The analysis and chart by themselves are not a story.

Contrast

Earlier in the chapter I told you about Ignaz Semmelweis. The data he had started out with was an example of contrast. The maternity clinic staffed by doctors and medical students had a much higher mortality due to childbed fever than the clinic staffed by midwives. That is the data. The 'why' behind that data is the story. The story of doctors and medical students doing autopsies, picking up something Semmelweis called 'cadaver particles' and then transmitting them to the mothers at the maternity clinic via their unwashed hands is the story.

Now, a few examples from the world of cricket. Arvind Iyengar and Rachit Agarwal from *Sportz Interactive* put together the information for the cricket stories. Joy Bhattacharjya and Boria Majumdar helped me understand the story behind the numbers. I am grateful to all of them.

Outliers

The scatterplot below plots all test bowlers who have taken 100 or more wickets in their career. The X-axis represents the number of wickets and the Y-axis represents the average number of runs given per wicket taken.

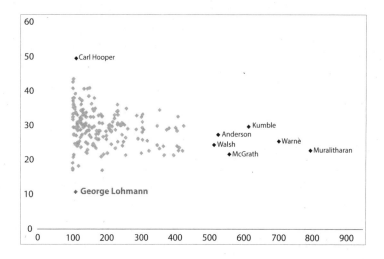

There are three sets of outliers: the 'rockstars' (Muttiah Muralitharan, Shane Warne, Anil Kumble, Glen McGrath, James Anderson, Courtney Walsh), the 'cringe worthy' (Carl Hooper), and the 'surprise' (George Lohmann).

I am sure that like me the average cricket fan must be saying, 'George Lohmann who?' Almost all regular followers of the game have heard of all the other names but not Lohmann. This got me Googling and here is what I found.

George Alfred Lohmann was born on 2 June 1865. He played first-class cricket in Surrey in 1884. In that year his place in the team was because of his promising batting. He bowled very little. It was the following year that was sensational. His haul of 142 first-class wickets made him the highest wicket taker that year. This got him into the English test side in 1886. While he had a dismal beginning taking just 1 wicket in the first test at Old Trafford and none in the second test in The Oval, he repaid the selectors faith by taking 12 wickets for 104 giving England what was one of the most decisive wins in the Ashes Series.

The next few years were glorious, even getting him the Wisden Cricketer of the Year award in 1889. However, he contracted tuberculosis in 1892. A partial recovery saw him back in first-class cricket in 1895.

In 1896, he was virtually unplayable. In three tests played on matting wickets he took 35 wickets for just 5.8 runs each. His deteriorating health and a pay dispute where he demanded double the standard rate saw him retire from test cricket in 1897. He died in 1901 aged only thirty-six. Now that is a story. A story I would have never unearthed if I hadn't seen this analysis and visualization.

Intersection

The One Day International (ODI) fortunes of two countries—West Indies and India—have almost mirrored each other. The figure below shows the two countries' ODI win percentages by decades.

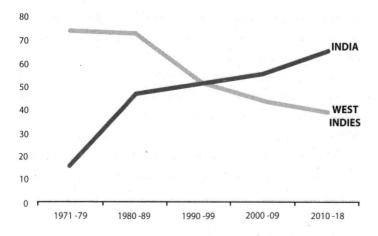

Passionate cricket followers born in any era and average cricket fans born in the 1970s would probably be able to name more West Indian crickets of the pre-2000 era than post-2000.

After reading several blogs and articles of cricket pundits, here are two possible 'Dream XI' team for the two countries.

West Indies: Gordon Greenidge, Conrad Hunt, George Headley, Vivian Richards, Brian Lara, Gary Sobers, Jackie Henricks, Malcolm Marshal, Micheal Holding, Curtly Ambrose and Lance Gibbs. (Interestingly, a few of the above were actually knighted.)

India: Sunil Gavaskar, Virender Sehwag, Rahul Dravid, Sachin Tendulkar, Vijay Hazare, Vinoo Mankad, Kapil Dev, M.S. Dhoni, Anil Kumble, Javagal Srinath and Erapalli Prasanna.

An interesting fact is that nine of the West Indies Dream XI retired before 1992 whereas seven of the Indian Dream XI started playing after 1992.

So, what created a coincidental decline in one country and rise in the other? A bit of research, a few conversations with cricket experts and historians allowed me to piece together this possible story.

The advent of ODIs brought about a dramatic change in the way cricket was played. The slower rhythm, orthodoxy and patience needed to be replaced with athleticism, innovation and aggression. The 1970s West Indies team under the captaincy of Clive Lloyd thrived in this situation.

The 1980s and 1990s saw a decline. Some of the causes that contributed to this were self-indulgence, lack of a unifier and the growth of basketball. After the successive victories in the ODI World Cup in 1975 and 1979, a belief that they were the undefeatable champions of the world created a sense of complacency in the West Indies cricket team. Many refer to West Indies as the smallest cricketing nation in the world. What remains hidden in that statement is that the West Indies cricket team is a sporting confederation of the Caribbean countries: Anguilla, Antigua and Barbuda, Barbados, Dominica, Grenada, Guyana, Jamaica, Montserrat, Saint Kitts and Nevis, Saint Lucia, Saint Vincent and the Grenadines, and Trinidad and Tobago. Keeping the team cohesive is a skill the captain of the West Indies cricket team required. A skill that seems to have been wanting in the captains after the departure of Clive Lloyd. The third factor is the rise of alternative sporting options. Driven by cable television and the attraction of scholarships, basketball started luring the top athletic talent coming out of school. The fact that the West Indies Cricket Board failed to adapt to the changing times and address the challenges made matters even worse.

It is during the same time that the opposite happened in India. India lead by Kapil Dev won the World Cup in 1983. The euphoria of the win followed by the explosion of cable television in the country during the late 1980s increased the following and glamourization of cricket in India. The God of Cricket—Sachin Tendulkar—played his first international game in 1989 and fired the imagination of every Indian school kid about the possibilities. These dreams and desires were supported ably by the dramatic professionalization of Indian cricket by the Board of Cricket Control in India (BCCI) under Jagmohan Dalmiya during the same period.

The figure at the beginning of this section shows the intersection of the two graphs for India and West Indies in the early 1990s. This is just data. But it provokes us to hunt and tell the story behind it.

As we have seen with the three examples above, analytic approaches can be used to discover stories that may be hidden in the data. A lot of this exploratory work involves trying multiple approaches. When one approach doesn't work, we need to backtrack and try another till one of them gives us a clue to a possible story.

The data you have may be of significant value, but none of that value will be extracted unless insights are uncovered and translated into actions or business results.

Storytelling with data is about doing just that.

Ethics and the Power of Stories

O N 10 OCTOBER 2013, O'connel street in downtown
Dublin was buzzing with tourists and people
leaving from work early. Near the post office,
a young woman stood out in the crowd. She seemed lost,
distressed and out of place.

A passer-by, concerned about her, called the police. The
police escorted her to the hospital and started questioning her.
There was a problem: she wasn't speaking.

A few days later, instead of words, she drew pictures. Using
stick figure drawings, she showed first being flown to Ireland on
an aeroplane. And then lying on a bed, surrounded by multiple
men. She seemed to be a victim of human trafficking—one of
the lucky ones who had somehow managed to escape.

The Irish authorities spent almost a month, over 2000
manhours exploring every possible line of inquiry, scanning
CCTV footage and missing peoples' list, conducting door-to-
door queries, checking hotel and hostel bookings, and visiting

airports, seaports and railway stations. But nothing yielded any information. Dubbed 'Operation Shepherd', the search had already cost them €250,000. The Irish National Police then decided to do something unprecedented, they distributed the girl's photograph publicly.

Initially, the newspapers and television broadcasts gave no positive results.

Then, they received a call. A man named Joe Brennan, who lived in a small town, about 170 km from Dublin, identified her as Samantha Azzopardi. Joe was Samantha's mother's former boyfriend. Samantha had decided to visit him and had flown in from Sydney. She was twenty-five years old.

A call to Interpol revealed that she was well known to them. Operating with more than forty aliases, she had conned authorities in many other countries. She had previously posed as an orphan, as a troubled gymnast from Russia, and a human trafficking victim, among others.

The Irish authorities awarded her a suspended prison sentence, a stern warning of never returning to Ireland and deported her.

A year later, she reappeared in Calgary, Canada. This time, her name was Aurora Hepburn, aged fifteen years. She used the same story of sex trafficking and abuse. This time, it cost the authorities $150,000.

Finally, in June 2017, the Australian authorities put Samantha, now twenty-eight, behind bars after she used the same story of sex trafficking at a Sydney High School, posing as thirteen-year-old Harper Hart. This lie had cost New South Wales authorities AUD155,000.

How did hard-nosed authorities around the world fall for her story?

This is because we are all susceptible to manipulation via stories. As authorities heard the story, their brain chemistry actually changed.

You may remember that in the introductory chapter we discussed Paul Zak. In his experiment, he demonstrated that emotionally charged stories cause oxytocin to be released into our blood stream, which can lead to unexpected behavioural changes, including profound acts of altruism.

The same chemical—oxytocin—became Samantha Azzopardi's ally.

Maria Konnikova, author of the book *The Confidence Game*,[1] says, 'Stories are so natural that we don't notice how much they permeate our lives. And stories are usually on our side: they are meant to delight us, not deceive us—an ever-present form of entertainment.'

She continues, 'That's precisely why they can be such a powerful tool of deception. When we're immersed in a story, we let our guard down. We focus in a way we wouldn't if someone were just trying to catch us with a random phrase or picture or interaction. In those moments of fully immersed attention, we may absorb things, under the radar, that would normally pass us by or put us on high alert.'

While I have often spoken about the power of stories to inspire and influence, there is always the other side of the coin. The power to manipulate.

In a 1978 speech, 'How to Build a Universe That Doesn't Fall Apart Two Days Later,'[2] Philip K. Dick had put this very succinctly. He said:

> The basic tool for the manipulation of reality is the manipulation of words. If you can control the meaning of words, you can control the people who must use the words.

We have been part of many games during leadership off-sites when as a group we have seen situational leadership, that at times some people take on the role of the leader depending on his or her areas of expertise. If we go back to those times and reflect on what made it evident to the other people in the team that following him or her was a good idea, we will see that it was what he said that persuaded us.

And hence, as storytellers, we must adhere to Spiderman's motto: with great power comes great responsibility.

But is all manipulation unethical?

When an entrepreneur is pitching to investors, he is definitely trying to influence the investor. Is that manipulation?

When a salesperson is trying to persuade potential customers to buy his or her product instead of someone else's, is that manipulation?

I think the dictionary definition of manipulation throws some light on this. The Oxford English Dictionary defines 'manipulate' as: 'to control or influence (a person or situation) cleverly or unscrupulously'. Dictionary.com defines it as: 'to manage or influence skilfully, especially in an unfair manner'.

The keywords in the above descriptions are 'unscrupulously' and 'unfair'. These are indeed very tough judgements to make as often we tell ourselves stories about why something we have done or are doing is fair.

So, what then is the North Star that should guide our being ethical in storytelling?

The same elements that guide each of us to be ethical in everything else that we do also apply to storytelling: honesty, integrity, fairness, concern for others, respect for others and accountability.

Shawn Callahan has some easy to follow guidelines when trying to ensure we don't end up manipulating.

In a blog post, he shared four tips to uphold the ethics of storytelling.

1. Tell stories as you believe they happened.
2. Tell people when you've made up a story.
3. Don't tell others' stories as if they are your own.
4. Protect confidentiality.

There are two tips I would like to add: don't tell a story that you wouldn't tell if the characters of the stories were present, and don't use stories to do anything that you wouldn't want others to do to you.

Having said all this, there are a few lies that I do allow myself. These lies were articulated very well by storytelling coach Matthew Dicks in a podcast.

1. **Lie of Omission:** When I leave out elements or information that are not central to the story and complicate the storyline, especially in very concisely told business stories.
2. **Lie of Assumption:** When I can't remember or don't know a detail of a story, such as what exactly a character in my story said to someone else or how the character

exactly felt in a situation, I make reasonable and plausible assumptions.

3. **Lie of Compression:** When I shift time or change location to achieve brevity and single-mindedness in the story I am sharing.

I know that you must be thinking of the same thing I am always hyper aware of: this is a slippery slope. When do these lies move from being acceptable to unacceptable? Here again, I think the dictionary comes to my rescue.

Dictionary.com defines 'lie' as 'a false statement made with deliberate intent to deceive; an intentional untruth; something intended to convey a false impression'. The filter for me is the intention. But these are indeed fine lines, and we must tread very carefully.

Yes, with great power, comes great responsibility.

The other responsibility leaders carry is to ensure that we don't tell only one side of the story. As author Chinua Achebe once said, 'Until the lions have their own historians, the history of the hunt will always glorify the hunter.'

There is a huge danger of a story from a single perspective.

Nigerian writer Chimamanda Adichie, in her brilliant TED talk 'The Dangers of a Single Story'[3] tells us about this risk. She says:

How they are told, who tells them, when they are told, how many stories are told, are really dependent on power. Power is the ability not just to tell the story of another person, but to make it the definitive story of that person.

She continues with:

> Start the story with the arrows of the Native Americans,
> but not with the arrival of the British, and you have an
> entirely different story. Start the story with the failure of
> the African states, and not with the colonial creation of the
> African state, and you have an entirely different story . . .

The single story creates stereotypes, and the problem with
stereotypes is not that they are untrue, but that they are
incomplete. They make one story become the only story.

It is our responsibility as leaders to seek out the truth and
not see just a single perspective, to seek out the fact and not
just have an opinion. As long as we do all the above to the best
of our abilities, with honesty, integrity and respect for others,
we can continue to harness the power of stories to connect,
engage, align and inspire.

18

Building a Sustainable
Storytelling Organization

Four years ago, when I started StoryWorks, a consulting and training firm focused on business storytelling, the task of selling the idea seemed to be uphill.

Given my credentials of a management degree from an IIM and twenty-one years of experience in organizations like Unilever, Tata and Mahindra, getting an appointment with corporates was not a very difficult task. But as soon as the conversation would start and I would mention about our focus on business storytelling, eyebrows would start rising. A fleeting smile would pass over the listener's face and inside his head he would say, 'and I thought this was going to be a serious discussion.'

This is not a unique experience. Twelve years ago, when Yamini Naidu, a fellow proponent of business storytelling from Australia, went to her mother and told her that she was starting a venture specializing in business storytelling, her mother said, 'Business storytelling? Is that even a job? Why can't you be a doctor or in IT? You can do storytelling on the weekends.'

The prevailing myth in business is that stories are usually made up, stories are for entertainment and stories are for children.

That myth is ingrained. As we discussed in the introductory chapter, anyone saying 'let me tell you a story' during a business conversation is usually met with rolling eyes and a retort of 'let's be serious'. That is the barrier stories face in business.

So, the first task we have in order to bring storytelling into the organization is to shatter this myth.

A great way to start is 'to be the change you want to see in the world'. Start using stories yourself but with those caveats— no using the 's' word, not too many details, no storytelling voice—to make a business point. Remember storytelling in business needs to be invisible.

Watch out for the next occasion when you catch yourself giving an opinion, something that is bound to happen on a daily basis. Choose an instance when the opinion you are going to share is one that you feel strongly about. It is certain that the opinion you have was formed due to some experience. Strong opinions are formed when either the experience had important consequences or when the experience had been repeated several times. Now, share your opinion and also share one of your experiences.

Here is an example. Imagine that I am about to share a very strong opinion about how new projects should be approached. I believe that strong project planning is the only way to guarantee success. I think a minimum of 20 per cent of the allotted time for the project needs to be spent in thinking about the problem, discussing approaches and weighing the pros and cons of each approach before taking a decision.

Surely, this is not a belief that I was born with. Something must have happened which made me have this belief. Perhaps I had jumped into executing an important project sometime in the past and discovered after a lot of work had gone into it that I was on the wrong track, and I rued the fact that I hadn't paused to plan. Or perhaps in a recent case, I did spend 20 per cent of my time thinking and planning and the project was very successfully completed. Often, if the opinion I have is very strong, I have had multiple experiences that shaped the belief.

Now, when I gather my team to tell them the importance of project planning, I would say, 'I believe a minimum of 20 per cent of the project time needs to be spent in deciding the approach.' I would make this assertion and add, 'Three years ago . . .' and narrate the incident that led me to have this belief.

You would probably start this in low-evaluation, low-judgement situations like discussions with the team that you lead or with peers. Once you are more confident, you must use it with senior leaders who might be critical of your agenda of bringing the power of storytelling into your organization. With this, you would be demonstrating the power of stories.

Another way to secure the senior management's buy-in is to have an expert in business storytelling come and deliver a keynote on harnessing the power of stories in business with a lot of real-life case studies. This way, in a short time, you would be exposing the decision makers, to the entire gamut of narrative work and the benefit of using stories at work.

Once you have the senior leadership's buy-in, here are a few steps you can follow.

Capability Building

The best way to drive change and get an organization to adopt a new behaviour is to go top-down. It is best to start with the CEO, the leadership team and key influencers from internal communication and human resources. Role modelling by senior leaders does wonders to drive change. Not only does the larger employee base have examples that they learn from, but they also understand how important this is to the organization.

It is important to find the right partner to build this skill. Unlike when I started, there is now a buzz around business storytelling. Everyone is calling themselves a storyteller, every company, product and service *must* have a story and there are many outfits offering business storytelling training. How do you choose the right one?

There are four key criteria for choosing the right partner. The first is: learn business storytelling from business people. Corporate experience matters because storytelling seems so foreign for many executives. They want to feel comfortable that they are being guided by someone like them who has done it before in similar circumstances. The second is: learn from storytellers. Anyone teaching business storytelling must be proficient at telling business stories. Storytelling is a craft learnt through imitation and practice. If during the pitch the prospective trainer's presentation is full of assertion and opinions and devoid of stories, clearly that is not a great choice.

The third is: focus on forming a storytelling habit. A single workshop doesn't change behaviour because storytelling is a habit that requires persistence and repetition to develop. Having a follow-up plan which brings the knowledge into practice at the workplace is essential. The fourth is: include coaching. Deliberate practice requires coaching. Students of storytelling benefit from timely feedback applied to real-world problems. Coaching helps participants get feedback on real business stories that they have used in real situations.

Introduce Storytelling Linked to a Key Business Issue

Skill building is best sustained when it is linked with the rollout of key business communications such as a new vision, a new strategy, new values, new leaders' behaviour expectations or some large transformation. When organizations create narratives for these key messages and use storytelling to share this with the organization, two powerful things happen. One: the skill learnt is put into practice and hence reinforced. Two: the communication success that usually follows this process drives adoption of this new behaviour across the organization.

Create a Process of Continuous Story Collection

Capturing stories from across the organization on key themes gets everybody involved and is probably the most pervasive way to build the story culture. The story collection is best linked to the key business issue chosen. If the organization chooses to communicate a new strategy or a transformation via a narrative, the stories being collected can be based on the key themes of that strategy or transformation. If the organization is looking at embedding values, the story collection would be around examples of these values in action across the organization.

The process should include employees from all parts of the business. Stories that come from various levels of the organization are usually seen to be more relatable and believable than stories that come just from the top. This also allows us to weave storytelling into the fabric of the organization. It creates a storytelling culture. Like I said before, isn't culture nothing but 'the way we do things here'?

Create a Story-Sharing Process

In order to get the benefit of storytelling, we must be telling these stories regularly and across the entire business. Having collected the stories, we must create a system through which we select the best stories and then broadcast them.

The most powerful way to share stories is orally and hence the best way to share these is to get the people who have been trained in storytelling to record these stories. One doesn't need fancy equipment for this. Our smartphones are very good audio and video recording devices. The recorded stories can then be put on the intranet, on the company's YouTube channel, pushed through WhatsApp groups, or shared on Facebook, etc.

My favourite way is to create a system where every monthly meeting of teams from across the organization starts with the best stories selected. This is not only a great form of recognition for the hero of the story but also creates peer pressure. It is good motivation for employees to display the required behaviour so that their stories too get selected.

Investing Resources to Run This Programme

This is where I have seen many companies falter. At a time when getting additional resources for important business projects seems difficult, very few people assign a dedicated resource to run the company's story process. This is a vital element. Creating any new behaviour is not easy and, very often, after the initial buzz, it is relegated as last month's flavour. A dedicated resource is required to keep the process going till it becomes a habit. As this happens, and as people see the benefit of this, storytelling will become a key component of the way your business works.

A vibrant storytelling culture creates the difference between an organization that has a living, breathing portfolio of different stories from different perspectives, which shares its impact—or just a single, somewhat stagnant story. It's the difference between having one person in the organization dedicated to storytelling (whether that's the CEO or the head of communications) and everyone in the organization having compelling stories on their fingertips.

19

Going Forward

I WAS PRACTISING in a bunker in Texas and this good old boy with a big hat stopped to watch. The first shot he saw me hit went in the hole. He said, 'You got 50 bucks if you knock the next one in.' I holed the next one. Then he says, 'You got $100 if you hole the next one.' In it went for three in a row. As he peeled off the bills, he said, 'Boy, I've never seen anyone so lucky in my life.' And I shot back, 'Well, the harder I practise, the luckier I get.

This is what golf legend Gary Player said in an interview with *Golf Digest* in 2002.[1]

We all know practice is crucial. We have all heard, in awe, the number of hours of practice a legend like Sachin Tendulkar put in even till his last cricket match. However, all of us have had the experience of not following up on our desire to learn a new skill: learning to play the guitar, learning a new language or learning to cook. What stopped us?

There are many barriers to learning. For instance, take my attempt at learning how to play the guitar. It took fifteen years of voicing intent before I bought one. But between my work and other demands at home, I rarely made time to practise. And even when I did find time to sit down and try and learn a few chords, I realized that there was no hope in hell that I would ever sound like my childhood idol, Mark Knopfler. And that was it. The guitar has now travelled with me through five house changes and still sits in a corner of my study, waiting for me to pick it up someday and start again.

What were the barriers?

1. **Casualness of Intent:** An effort at learning something voluntarily, just for the sake of learning, rarely lasts long. I hadn't articulated clearly why I wanted to learn to play the guitar. Hence, it became impossible to prioritize it over other items on my checklist, which often included catching up on sleep, catching up with friends or catching up with the missed episodes of *Game of Thrones*.

2. **Not Setting Realistic Milestones:** My initial target was clearly not mastering the skill or becoming an expert. However, comparing myself with experts in the field made the contrast intimidating. This incorrect comparison led to frustration with my initial lack of finesse. I somehow didn't budget for the fact that I would initially be terrible at anything new. Very soon, I felt stupid, and since I hadn't clearly articulated why I wanted to learn to play the guitar, I stopped. I quickly convinced myself that it wasn't important in the first place.

3. **Not Setting up Stakes:** I hadn't identified a time in the near future where I would demonstrate my ability to play. I hadn't announced my intent even to myself. Since there was no consequence if I gave up, it was easy to do so.

Taking some lessons from this, I would now like you to take a little time and answer the following questions. You could either use this page or any note-taking device on your phone or laptop. But I do want you to put it down as I am sure you will need to revisit it.

1. Why do I want to use storytelling in my work? (Instead of something very vague like 'because I want to be a more impactful communicator', put down things that are specific. This could include things like 'I want to be able to increase the number of times I can get my ideas across to my department head', or, 'I want to be able to inspire my team to deliver on their yearly goals, etc.').

   _____

   _____

   _____

2. Come up with a concrete plan. When are you going to practise? (An hour every Sunday or thirty minutes every Monday and Thursday).

   _____

   _____

   _____

3. Create stakes. Identify at least two occasions of consequence where you will use a story or story structures in the near future. (A town hall next month where you will speak about the work being done by your team or a proposal presentation to a client next month.)

_____

_____

_____

4. For each of the above situations, which story pattern will you use (connection, clarity, influence or success).

_____

_____

_____

Now, let us move on to how we would practise the above.

Practice doesn't make you perfect. Only perfect practice makes you perfect. Quality of practice is just as important as the quantity. It seems obvious when you think about it. I could play badminton every evening with my neighbours, but that would not help me qualify for any competitive event. To be an expert, I would need to design a highly structured activity with the specific goal of improving performance. So, for one week I would only practise smashes. I may even record my smashes and view them to understand what I should work on based on the techniques I learn either from a coach or from a YouTube tutorial. Then I would practise again by incorporating the changes I need to. Having become much better at smashes, the next week, I could focus on drop shots. Just drop shots. Again, the same cycle is repeated—practise, record, view, correct, practise. This is definitely different from a simple repetition of a task: playing badminton every day. We need to design and perform a programme of activities focused on developing specific skills. The difference is graphically depicted in the diagram below.

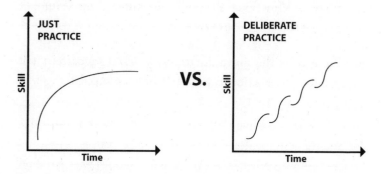

Simple practice isn't enough to rapidly gain skills. Mere repetition of an activity won't lead to improved performance. Practice must be intentional, aimed at improving performance, designed for your current skill level, combined with immediate feedback, and repetitive. It is important to note that without adequate feedback, efficient learning is impossible and improvement is minimal.

Now, let us translate this to the plan you put down earlier. You will be surprised what a recording can do to your delivery. Just an audio recording.

When you listen to a speech, can you say if it was interesting or boring? Can you judge whether the speaker made an impact or not? Can you at the end of the speech tell me whether the speaker knows about the subject or not? If the speaker were to reach out to you and ask for feedback, would you be able to do a fairly good job? Of course, the answer to all four questions must be a vehement 'yes!' Then why is it that you can't make these critical judgements about your own speech or presentation? It is only because you don't hear yourself delivering them with an objective ear.

Here is something that will guarantee a minimum of 50 per cent improvement in your delivery. Take your smartphone. Put it into flight mode so that there are no interruptions. Start an audio recording app. Place the phone upside down on the table or podium in front of you. Deliver. Later that day, listen to the recording and jot down the areas that need improvement. Practise the corrected version out loud within the confines of your home or office. The usual process follows: practise, record, listen, correct, practise. You will be surprised at the dramatic improvement you see.

Now take a look at the stakes you had in mind and the story patterns you decided to use in each of the situations. Create your story for each type using the tools and techniques you learnt about in this book and then practise, record, view, correct and practise.

In his book *Talent is Overrated*,[2] Geoff Colvin asserts that high performers are not necessarily naturally talented, but they engage in deliberate practice.

There is a beautiful story in the book about how Benjamin Franklin developed a programme to improve his writing skills. Colvin writes that Franklin would read the *Spectator*, a popular English periodical of that era, and would locate prose that was clearly superior to his own. He would then follow an amazing process. He would first make brief notes about the meaning of each sentence, then wait for a few days and use his own words to express the meaning. He would then compare the completed essay written in his words to that of the original. This comparison helped him discover some of his faults and correct them. In the story, Colvin goes on to describe an even more complex step that followed.

> One of the faults he noticed was his poor vocabulary. What could he do about that? He realized that writing poetry required an extensive 'stock of words' because he might need to express any given meaning in many different ways depending on the demands of rhyme or meter. So he would rewrite *Spectator* essays in verse. Then, after he had forgotten them, he would take his versified essays and rewrite them in prose, again comparing his efforts with the original.

What an involved process. But as they say: no pain, no gain.

So, as you decide to embark on the journey to becoming a powerful business storyteller, or indeed acquire any new skill, keep in mind the requirement of deliberate practice and build that element into your programme. Remember: an expert at anything was a beginner once.

So go ahead and embark on the extremely rewarding storytelling journey and build your reputation as a storyteller, one story at a time.

NOTES

Introduction: The Art of Gathering Gold Dust

1. J.A. Barraza and P.J. Zak, 'Empathy toward Strangers Triggers Oxytocin Release and Subsequent Generosity', Annals of the New York Academy of Science, 1167, pp. 182–89, 2009.
2. Jim Collins and Jerry I. Porras, *Built to Last: Successful Habits of Visionary Companies* (New York: HarperBusiness, 1997).
3. J.P. Kotter and J.L. Heskett, *Corporate Culture and Performance* (New York: Free Press, 1992).
4. K. Robinson and L. Aronica, *The Element: How Finding Your Passion Changes Everything* (New York: Penguin Group USA, 2009).

Chapter 1: Stories Are Powerful: Evolution and Biology Have a Role to Play

1. K.F. Haven, *Story Proof: The Science behind the Startling Power of Story* (Santa Barbara, CA: Libraries Unlimited, 2007).
2. J. S. Bruner, *Acts of Meaning* (Cambridge, Massachusetts: Harvard University Press, 1998).
3. K.F. Haven, *Story Smart: Using the Science of Story to Persuade, Influence, Inspire, and Teach* (Santa Barbara, CA: Libraries Unlimited, 2014).

4.   S. Pinker, *The Language Instinct* (New York: Perennial Classic, 2000); F. Crick and C. Koch, 'Are We Aware of Neural Activity in the Primal Visual Cortex?', *Nature*, 375: 121–23, 1995, https://go.nature.com/2KhAFNB., H. Newquist, *The Great Brain Book* (New York: Scholastic Reference, 2004), R. Kotulak, *Inside the Brain: Revolutionary Discoveries of How the Mind Works* (Kansas City, MO: Andrews McNeal, 1999).

5.   Dr John Medina, *Brain Rules: 12 Principles for Surviving and Thriving at Work, Home, and School* (Seattle, WA: Pear Press, 2008).

6.   G.J. Stephens, L.J. Silbert and U. Hasson, 'Speaker-Listener Neural Coupling Underlies Successful Communication', Proceedings of the National Academy of Science (USA), 107(32) 14425–30, 2010.

7.   G. Di Pellegrino, L. Fadiga, L. Fogassi, V. Gallese, G. Rizzolatti, 'Understanding Motor Events: A Neurophysiological Study'; Ncbi.nlm.nih.gov, 91:176–80, 1991, https://bit.ly/2Iy9Mb9.

8.   J. Gonzalez, A. Barros-Loscertales, F. Pulvermuller, V Meseguer, Ana Sanjuan, Vicente Belloch, Cesar Avila, et al,. 'Reading *Cinnamon* Activates Olfactory Brain Regions, *NeuroImage*, 32:906–12, 2006, https://bit.ly/2IGyciu.

Chapter 2: Why Stories?

1.   J.M. Mandler, *Stories, Scripts, and Scenes: Aspects of Schema Theory* (Hillsdale, N. J: L. Erlbaum Associates, 1984).

2.   P. Guber, 'The Four Truths of the Storyteller', *Harvard Business Review*, 2007, https://bit.ly/1S6TjtH.

Chapter 5: Using Stories to Build Rapport and Credibility

1.   S. Sinek, 'Simon Sinek: How Great Leaders Inspire Action', https://bit.ly/OX0t5a, 2009.

2.   S. Denning, *The Leader's Guide to Storytelling: Mastering the Art and Discipline of Business Narrative* (San Francisco: Jossey-Bass/A Wiley Imprint, 2009).

3. S. Crainer and D. Dearlove, *Generation Entrepreneur: Shape Today's Business Reality, Create Tomorrow's Wealth, Do Your Own Thing* (London: Financial Times Management, 2000).

4. J. Gottschall, *The Storytelling Animal: How Stories Make Us Human* (New York: Mariner Books, 2013).

5. S. Sinek, 'Simon Sinek: If You Don't Understand People, You Don't Understand Business', https://adobe.ly/2rH8kJy, 2012.

6. I. Nooyi, 'Aspen Ideas Festival, In Conversation: Indra Nooyi and David Bradley', https://bit.ly/2rJnOMi, 2014.

Chapter 6: Using Stories to Influence and Overcome Objections

1. Denise Cummings, *Good Thinking: Seven Powerful Ideas That Influence the Way We Think* (Cambridge University Press, 2012).

Chapter 7: Getting Strategies to Stick

1. Robert Kaplan and David Norton, *The Strategy-Focused Organization: How Balanced Scorecard Companies Thrive in the New Business Environment* (Boston: Harvard Business Review, 2000).

2. E. J. Langer, A. Blank and B. Chanowitz, 'The Mindlessness of Ostensibly Thoughtful Action: The Role of "Placebic" Information in Interpersonal Interaction', Journal of Personality and Social Psychology, 36(6), 635–42 (1978).

3. Elizabeth Newton, 'Overconfidence in the Communication of Intent: Heard and Unheard Melodies', PhD dissertation, Stanford University, 1990.

4. A. Simmons, *Whoever Tells the Best Story Wins: How to Use Your Own Stories to Communicate with Power and Impact* (New York: AMACOM, 2015).

Chapter 9: Story Listening

1. David Isay and Maya Millet, 'Calling: The Purpose and Passion of Work' (New York: Penguin Press, 2016).
2. Hailan Hu, et al., 'Emotion Enhances Learning via Norepinephrine Regulation of AMPA-Receptor Trafficking', *Cell*, 131, 160–73 (2007).

Chapter 10: Getting Values to Be Understood, Remembered and Put into Action

1. 'The Ritz-Carlton: A Tradition of Storytelling', https://bit.ly/2hMXYp1.

Chapter 11: Understanding Complex Human Issues by Listening to Stories

1. David J. Snowden and Mary E. Boone, 'A Leader's Framework for Decision Making', *Harvard Business Review*, 85, 68–76, 149, 2007.

Chapter 12: Other Powerful Uses of Story Listening

1. David W. De Long, *Lost Knowledge: Confronting the Threat of an Aging Workforce* (England: Oxford University Press, 2004).
2. D.F. Frank, R.P. Finnegan and C.R. Taylor, 'The Race for Talent: Retaining and Engaging Workers in the 21st Century', Human Resource Planning, 12–25, 2004.
3. E.A. Smith, 'The Role of Tacit and Explicit Knowledge in the Workplace', *Journal of Knowledge Management*, 5, 311–21, 2001.
4. Excerpt from a five-page letter I had written during my management trainee programme at Hindustan Unilever in 1992.
5. G.A. Klein, *Seeing What Others Don't: The Remarkable Ways We Gain Insights* (Boston: Nicholas Brealey Publishing, 2013).

Chapter 13: Managing Change through Stories

1. J.P. Kotter, 'Leading Change: Why Transformation Efforts Fail', Harvard Business Review, 73, 259–267, 1995.
2. F. Reichheld, *The Ultimate Question 2.0: How Net Promoter Companies Thrive in a Customer-Driven World* (Boston: Harvard Business Review Press, 2011).

Chapter 14: Storytelling for the Super Salesman

1. D. Brown, *The Da Vinci Code: A Novel* (New York: Doubleday, 2003).
2. C.G. Lord, L. Ross and M.R. Lepper, 'Biased Assimilation and Attitude Polarization: The Effects of Prior Theories on Subsequently Considered Evidence', *Journal of Personality and Social Psychology*, 37(11), 2098–109, 1979.

Chapter 15: Presentation and Storytelling

1. R. Elias, '3 Things I Learned While My Plane Crashed', https://bit.ly/2rNh0xB, 2011.
2. J. Oliver, 'Teach Every Child about Food', https://bit.ly/1oYzeTB, 2010.
3. H. Rosling, 'The Magic Washing Machine', https://bit.ly/1NnVjpd.
4. A. Cuddy, *Presence: Bringing Your Boldest Self to Your Biggest Challenges* (New York: Little, Brown and Company, Hachette Book Company, 2015).
5. A. Cuddy, 'Your Body Language May Shape Who You Are', https://bit.ly/1gENuLB, 2012.
6. B. Brown, 'The Power of Vulnerability', https://bit.ly/1lJtLD1, 2010.
7. J. Campbell, *The Hero with a Thousand Faces* (Princeton, N.J.: Princeton University Press, 2004).

8. C. Vogler, *The Writer's Journey: Mythic Structure for Writers* (Studio City, CA: M. Wiese Productions, 1998).

9. N. Duarte, *Resonate: Present Visual Stories that Transform Audiences* (Hoboken, N.J.: Wiley, 2010).

10. Z. Ebrahim, 'I Am the Son of a Terrorist, Here's How I Chose Peace', https://bit.ly/1rACc08.

Chapter 16: Storytelling with Data

1. 'Meet the Fire Hydrant that Unfairly Nets NYC $25,000 a year', I QuantNY.com, https://bit.ly/1vmfGAG.

2. I. Semmelweis, Wikipedia.com, https://bit.ly/1YVaD3F.

3. S. Johnson, *The Ghost Map: The Story of London's Most Terrifying Epidemic—and How It Changed Science, Cities, and the Modern World* (New York: Riverhead Books, 2006).

Chapter 17: Ethics and Power of Stories

1. M. Konnikova, *The Confidence Game: Why We Fall for It . . . Every Time* (USA: Penguin Books, 2017).

2. P.K. Dick and L. Sutin, *The Shifting Realities of Philip K. Dick: Selected Literary and Philosophical Writings* (New York: Pantheon Books, 1995).

3. Chimamanda Adichie, 'The Danger of a Single Story', https://bit.ly/1kMOnud, 2009.

Chapter 19: Going Forward

1. G. Yocom, 'My Shot: Gary Player', *Golf Digest*, August 2010, https://www.golfdigest.com/story/myshot_gd0210.

2. G. Colvin, *Talent is Overrated: What Really Separates World-Class Performers from Everybody Else* (New York, Penguin Portfolio).